# 51 Pioneer Scientists of India

(Life-stories of Epoch-making Scientists of India)



**Prakash Manu**

*Sahitya Akademi's first Children's Literature Award-winning author*

DIAMOND BOOKS

www.diamondbook.in

**Publisher** : **Diamond Pocket Books (P) Ltd.**
X-30, Okhla Industrial Area, Phase-II
New Delhi-110020
Phone : 011-40712200
E-mail : sales@dpb.in
Website : www.diamondbook.in
Edition : 2023

---

**51 Pioneer Scientists of India**
*Author : Prakash Manu*

***Dedicated to***

Dr. Shanti Swaroop Bhatnagar,
the great scientist of India, who dreamed of
industrial revolution in a scientific way.

# 51 Pioneer Scientists of India

Like religion and spirituality, India has been on top worldwide in mathematics and science as well, and today again it is marking a distinguished identity on the map of the whole world. There are a few countries that can match to it in IT i.e. 'Information Technology' and today India has become a superpower in the world in this field. In ancient India, physicians like Charaka, Sushruta, Jivaka and amazing alchemists like Nagarjuna were world famous and scientists like Aryabhatt, Varahamihir, Brahmagupt and Bhaskaracharya made astonishing discoveries in science as well as mathematics. Today everyone accepts India's great contribution in this direction. Similarly, the invention of 'zero' is such a discovery of India, which has opened the door to the latest discoveries in science and mathematics.

In this book, a well-known litterateur and science-thinker Prakash Manu has told about the life and great contribution of 51 such pioneer scientists of India, by reading which the child and adolescent readers will get to know about the great scientific tradition of their country. At the same time, a dream and a new courage will arise within them to come forward and do something new in this field.

**Prakash Manu**

**Born:** May 12, 1950, in Shikohabad, Uttar Pradesh.

**Education:** Prakash Manu, who lived life in his own unique way, was a brilliant student of science. After getting M.Sc. in Physics from Agra College, Agra, the course of his life changed due to interest in literature. He was associated with the editing of the popular children's magazine '*Nandan*' for twenty-five years. He is now a completely freelance writer, working on some big plans related to children's literature.

**Novel:** *Yeh Jo Dilli Hai, Katha Circus, Papa Ke Jaane Ke Baad.*

**Stories**: *21 Shreshta Kahaniyan, Mrs. Majumdar, Zindagi Nama Ek Genius Ka, Arundhati Udaas Hai, Tum Kahan Ho Naveen Bhai, Socrates Mere Shahar Mein, Uncle Ko Wish Nahi Karoge.*

**Poetry:** *Ek Aur Prarthana, Chhootata Hua Ghar, Kavita aur Kavita ke Beech.*

**Children's Literature**: 51 funny stories for children, amazing stories of knowledge-science, 51 amazing stories of Matunga forest, 51 pleasing stories of fairies, unique stories of Tenaliram's cleverness, chin-chin choon, *Nandu Bhaiya Ki Patange* (stories), *Golu Bhaga Ghar Se, Ek Tha Thunthuniya, Chinnu's Zoo, Little Gogo's Adventures, Khukkan Dada's Childhood* (Novel), *Hathi Ka Juta, Ekyavan Bal Kavitayen* (Poems). He did work of historical importance by writing *Hindi Bal Kavita Ka Itihaas* which is the first systematic history of children's poetry in Hindi. Apart from this, he did some distinct work in memoirs, interviews and criticism; he edited many important books as well.

**Award:** Sahitya Akademi's first Children's Literature Award and Hindi Academy's 'Literary Award'. First Girijakumar Mathur Smriti Award for the collection of poems *'Chhootata Hua Ghar'*.

**Address:** 545, Sector-29, Faridabad- 121008 (Haryana)

**Mobile:** 09810602327

*Preface*

# India's Pioneer Scientists

The whole world sees and knows India as a great spiritual country. But like religion and spirituality, India has been a top country in mathematics and science as well and today again it is marking a different identity on the map of the whole world. There is no substitute to it in IT i.e. Information Technology and today India has become a superpower in the world in this field. Today the whole world has started believing that Indians have no dearth of talent and excellence and if they get the right tools, they can do extraordinary things. For a long time in our country, scientists had to do their work and research in utter resource crunch. So they went abroad and there their extraordinary inventions attracted the attention of the whole world. Har Govind Khorana is one such Indian scientist who opened doors of new research in the whole world in terms of genetics i.e. gene structure. Similarly, Subrahmanyan Chandrasekhar attracted the attention of scientists from all over the world with his explanation of black holes in the universe structure. Earlier, a great genius scientist of India, Dr. Satyendra Nath Bose had the privilege of working with Einstein and Einstein himself used to appreciate his talent.

Instruments with which India's first Nobel laureate scientist Raman used to explain the effect of light rays to prove his Raman Effect were not extraordinary devices. Through intensive investigation with the help of very simple equipment, he put forward an extraordinary theory, which was accepted with great respect by scientists all over the world. Thus the great Indian scientist Raman proved that the great thing is not the means, but the great vision, and if it is there, great things can be done even with modest instruments.

Raman went abroad to attend a scientific conference, so while returning from there in a ship, there was only one confusion in his mind that where does this blue color come from in the sea? He was remembering the explanation of some great scientists about this, in which one thesis was that the blue color of the sea is actually the shadow of the sky. That is why the sea appears blue. But this explanation of the blueness of the sea water did not suit him much. Then where does this blueness in sea water come from? This dilemma one day took him to a big achievement like the Nobel Prize.

Similarly, Jagdishchandra Basu's belief that trees, plants and vegetation also have life and sensitivity was ridiculed earlier. But he proved it through scientific instruments and today all scientists believe it. Radio was also invented by Basu, an exceptionally talented scientist, but he could not patent it; this is also an accepted fact. The work and fame of Prafulla Chandra Ray in Chemistry, Birbal Sahni in Paleobotany and Srinivasa Ramanujan in Mathematics have also been in constant international discussions.

Similarly, Dr. Bhabha started thinking seriously about nuclear energy many decades ago and started working on big plans. If seen, it has a big role in India becoming a superpower. It was Dr. Bhabha who first spread India's message to the whole world that if atomic energy is used for peaceful and development works, then the face of our world can change and prosperity can come in every house. That is why Nehru ji used to praise Dr. Bhabha so much. He told Dr. Bhabha that for whatever he needed, instead of going to the government machinery and officials, he should directly ask him and Dr. Bhabha was also so engrossed in his work that his talent was visible to the whole world. Even when Nehru ji asked him to accept the post of minister, he flatly refused saying that he would be able to serve the country better only as a scientist. He was such a big and accomplished scientist that the post of minister had no meaning for him.

After the untimely and unfortunate demise of Dr. Bhabha, the name of Vikram Sarabhai is very important amongst the scientists of India who helped this country to emerge rapidly and make its place on the scientific scene of the world.

He set up an organization like ISRO for space research, which has achieved NASA-like importance in India's space research. This is the reason that today India was able to send its vehicle to the moon and is working on such big and ambitious plans in this field that it is expected that in a few years, India will be counted among the leading scientific talent-rich countries in this field.

Similarly, Dr. Shanti Swaroop Bhatnagar, who had dreamed of industrial progress in India with the help of science, really made a revolution. In terms of social development and human happiness and prosperity, the uses of science were seriously considered afresh and our country became a self-sufficient and powerful country in many respects. Undoubtedly, this role of science is not over yet and in this direction a big goal and big challenges are in front of us and it is expected that the scientists of our country will achieve their aim here too. In this sense, many of our institutes have achieved international fame through their continuous researches and activism. Similarly, the works of Salim Ali in Ornithology, Dr. Darasha Naushervan Wadia in Geology and Venu Bappu in Astronomy do not need any introduction. Former President of India Dr. A.P.J. Abdul

Kalam, with his new vision, has again established India on the world-science map with full pride.

If we discuss the ancient scientific development of India, then the achievements of our great sages-scientists are probably even more astonishing. The most surprising thing is that the ancient sages and scientists of India had so much and accurate information about our body, universe, planet-constellations and space without any special means that today's scientists can also learn a lot from them. Hundreds of years ago, with much labor and diligence they collected this information and handed it over to the next generations after analyzing and testing it. It itself proves that our sages and scientists of that era had such a strong hunger for the acquisition of knowledge. And as if they were engaged in knowing the secrets of the universe like a penance day and night. In this context, their discovery from generation to generation really revealed such differences of human existence and creation, due to which rapid development of human civilization took place. For example, earlier it was believed that solar and lunar eclipses occur due to the influence of Rahu and Ketu.

But then our ancient scientists like Aryabhatta removed this superstition and explained it completely scientifically that a lunar eclipse occurs when the Earth comes between the Sun and the Moon. Similarly, he explained the solar eclipse, which is unanimously accepted by all the scientists today. In this way, along with the scientific development, the misconceptions and superstitions stuck with us for centuries were removed and new scientific tools were made, which made our life happy and convenient.

Among the ancient scientists of India, Medhatithi is probably the oldest sage, who had amazing knowledge of counting a large number of numbers. They count bricks and cows and reach *parardha*, which means 1012. At that time people in the whole world could not count more than one lakh i.e. 105, but the Indian creators of Vedas had reached far and wide in this field with their deep thinking and their achievements still amaze us. Similarly, the unique concept of Yoga that Patanjali presented is completely scientific and derived from a very deep understanding of physiology. This is the reason that even after thousands of years have passed; its importance has not diminished. Even in today's modern culture when man's activities have increased a lot, the importance of Patanjali's yoga is known somewhere. If we focus on our energy, then we can do the biggest tasks of the world very easily. In this context, yoga is not only helpful in spiritual progress, but it is also very helpful in doing all our tasks smoothly and in arranging our life. This is the reason why not only in India, but also in the western world today, Indian Yoga is being propagated. Even in the twenty-first century, the whole world seems very eager to learn Pranayama and Yoga, so that we can get rid of the stresses of our everyday life and lead a blissful life.

The principles discovered by the sages and scientists of ancient India regarding the creation of universe, while continuously contemplating and churning, are also of great importance. Among the ancient sages of India, Kanad was a wonderful thinker who gave a unique explanation of the universe with the help of particle theory. To be honest, Kanad is the Adi Acharya of that atomism, which is still being spoken in the twenty-first century and new discoveries are still going on in this direction.

Similarly, in medical science, India had grown a lot since ancient times and such surgeries were done at that time, which is surprising to think about. In these there are also operations like operation of human brain and plastic surgery. Apart from this, the scientists of that period had extraordinary knowledge about the structure of the human body. Even the fairly accurate information about the human digestive and respiratory systems, circulation of blood and the total number of bones in the body were known at that time; for that they would have to dissect the body with their very simple looking tools. But they succeeded because their vision was completely scientific and their brilliant passion for discovering something new at every moment had no limit.

In this context, Jivaka, Charaka and Sushruta are such bright diamonds of Indian medical science, whose talents can hardly be seen anywhere else in the world. But the ideal of all these three great medical scientists was human service, which shows how different Indian life-view is from others and here science is also not for mere material progress. Rather, it is also inspired by moral values and is helpful in the spiritual progress of man. Later on, wonderful alchemists and great medical scientists like Nagarjuna, Vagbhatt, Madhavkar, Dradhbal, Vrinda and Bhavamishra took this tradition a long way and this wealth of Indian knowledge and science reached many countries of the world. The scientists there have gratefully accepted this debt of India.

How much India had progressed in science centuries ago can be gauged from this that the foundations given by Aryabhatta regarding Sun, Moon, Earth, Space etc. in his time still amaze us. He was thinking so ahead of his time that not only his contemporaries, but also many scientists who came after him opposed him. The view of Aryabhatta that the Sun does not revolve around the Earth, but the Earth revolves around the Sun, was not acceptable to anyone. Even great scientists like Varahamihir were not ready to accept that the Earth is not stable and it revolves around the Sun continuously.

He scoffed at the concept. But Aryabhatta was right and today scientists of the whole world accept how revolutionary his thoughts were.

Similarly, what scientists like Varahamihir, Brahmagupta and Bhaskaracharya made discoveries regarding science as well as mathematics, amaze us. Along with arithmetic, their knowledge and extraordinary erudition of geometry and algebra is surprising. Like algebra, India is the country that gave birth to trigonometry or trigonometry, whose words like 'jya' later changed to 'sine'. The great mathematicians of the world accept the great contribution of India in this direction. Similarly, the invention of zero is such a discovery of India, which opened the door to the latest discoveries in science and mathematics. If zero was not invented, then it is certain that today we would not have been able to use even computers. Because in the technical language of the computer, zero is a big component by which it registers things in its memory and identifies them.

Not only this, but the scientists of India very ahead in gaining expertise in every field of life. Horses were widely used in ancient times and there were thousands of horses in the stables of the kings. Shalihotra has given amazing information about the nature of horses, the test of good quality horses and their diseases in his book. Similarly, Bhoj Narhari has given such accurate scientific information about the extremely huge water vessels of India, their various advanced types, their construction and the wood and other things used in them, that we are amazed after reading it. It is understood by reading this that in this field also India had achieved a great achievement and expertise in ancient times and was far ahead of other countries of the world. Famous world traveler Marco Polo has also mentioned the huge ships of India's water and the trade through them.

In this book, the life and great contribution of such 51 Pioneer Scientists of India has been told, by reading which children and adolescent readers will know about the great scientific tradition of India. At the same time, a dream and a new courage will arise within them to come forward and do something new in this field. Letters from readers will be awaited.

**–Prakash Manu**

# Contents

# 1

# Medhatithi

## The pinnacle of ancient science (1500 BC)

Medhatithi's name is taken with great respect among the oldest scientific thinkers of India. Medhatithi was an ancient sage, whose hymns are found in Rigveda, Yajurveda and Atharvaveda. Thus, in these Vedic hymns, God and the deities have been praised. But the main thing is that many of the verses of Medhatithi are such that they show that he had a lot of knowledge of arithmetic.

In ancient India, these are the amazing verses of arithmetic, which shows how much India was ahead in the field of knowledge-science even in that period. Today, the Indian method of writing from one to ten trillion, Medhatithi was not only using it beautifully in the Vedic period, but was also able to compose beautiful poetry on its basis. In this context, Medhatithi can be called 'the first discoverer of Indian mathematics or numbers'.

In Yajurveda, a shloka has been given in the name of Medhatithi, in which counting has been done through bricks. The joy of playing with numbers or counting is unique in this verse. Climbing up step by step with the help of numbers, that is, this verse can definitely be called unique because of this count or table with the product of ten. The meaning of this beautiful verse of prayer is-

"O Lord of Fire, these bricks are like my milch cow. Let another ten become, Hundred (100), One thousand (1000), Ten thousand (10000), One lakh (100000), Ten lakh (1000000), One crore (10000000) Ten Crore (100000000), a sea (1000000000), a middle (10000000000) and an end (100000000000) and prarardha (1000000000000). May these bricks be my own milch cows in this world and the next world."

This shows that Medhatithi had knowledge about zero. He knew very well that by increasing one zero the value of the number increases. Increasingly, he had taken the number up to ten billion, which means one prayer in scientific terminology. If written then one prarardha would mean, 10 to the power of 12, i.e. 1012. Nowhere in the world were people familiar with such a large count at that time. They could count up to a thousand, ten thousand or a lakh, but not more than that. That is, up to 105 the mathematicians of the world were familiar, while Medhatithi, Vedic sage and mathematician of India, was counting very well till 1012.

Yes, there is definitely a limit to Medhatithi and his time that the method of writing such large numbers in numbers did not come into vogue at that time. Small numbers were written down by lines or some other signs, but large numbers were still written in words. Yet Medhatithi has used numbers so correctly and precisely in his verses that it would not be wrong to call him the inventor of Indian mathematics and numbers. Thousands of years ago, Medhatithi is the most ancient glory of the extraordinary perfection India achieved in arithmetic.

# 2

# Patanjali

## Great Master of Yoga Vidya (200 BC)

Patanjali was the great inventor of Yoga Vidya. In this form his fame is immortal and keeps on increasing. Even before Patanjali, discussions or sources about Yoga are found in the Vedas and Upanishads, but Patanjali did the unprecedented work of bringing out the essence of the entire Indian thought and knowledge about Yoga in one place. Not only this, Patanjali gave such completeness to his Yoga Book by bringing out the sources scattered here and there in the Upanishads and other ancient texts about Yoga, that even as some twenty-two centuries have passed but its relevance has not diminished even today.

Patanjali's most important discovery regarding yoga is that the peace of mind of a man is directly related to his breathing. We often see that when a person is calm, his breathing is moving at an even pace. But in moments of anger or passion, the speed of breath also changes and intensity, imbalance and irritation start appearing in that too. Therefore, the most important establishment of Patanjali's yoga-philosophy is that if a man's breath is controlled, it can change his state of mind. And if the state of mind becomes good, then it also has a good effect on the health of a person. That is, through yoga, a person can get health benefits even without any external medicine or medicine. Not only this, but by controlling the rate of breathing through yoga, one gradually rises to higher and higher states of consciousness and ultimately attains God or true spiritual realization.

According to Patanjali, this condition of the human mind or brain can be explained with the example of a pond. Like the wind playing with the water of the pond, in the same way many unnecessary thoughts arise in the mind. Then, from the ambush of those thoughts, new thoughts are born one after the other. If the powers of the mind are concentrated in meditation by stopping these unnecessary thoughts, then like a pearl lying in the calm water at the bottom of the pond, we can find God and true divine knowledge.

This philosophy of Patanjali about Yoga appeals to us more today because today's man has lost his peace of mind in the race for comforts. This peace cannot be achieved by external means or medicines. We can achieve this within ourselves through yoga. In this context, Patanjali is our guru and guide even today.

Apart from this, a major task of Patanjali was to compose a commentary on Charak's book *Charak Samhita.* Even today, this work of Patanjali is highly respected, so that Charak's medical ideas could come to us more clearly.

❐

# 3

# Shalihotra

## Globally renowned veterinarian of ancient times (800 BC)

Shalihotra's name is also well-known among the ancient medical scientists of India. The specialty of Shalihotra was that he was a well-known veterinary doctor of his time. Especially his information about horses and their diseases is so unique and complete that even today Shalihotra's book is mentioned with great respect all over the world. This may sound strange today. But the truth is that our knowledge of animal medicine (veternary scinece) was much more advanced in ancient times than it is today. Perhaps because horses, elephants or other animals were not only useful to humans, but humans also had a kind of romantic relationship with them. Today in the machine age that relationship has been changed. That's why earlier man used to worry about animals or their diseases etc. or used to think with great affection, today it is not the same. That's why veterinary medicine is going backward today. The knowledge of common people about them is also less today than before. In this context, the importance of Shalihotra and his book increases much more.

Today, we do not have much information about Shalihotra's life. He is said to have been the son of a Brahmin sage Hayaghosha and lived in Shravasti. He is said to be contemporary of Sushruta and Agnivesh. In this context, Shalihotra happened in the eighth century BC, that is, some 2800 years ago.

Shalihotra's knowledge of horses was so unique that his fame had spread far and wide. He has given a detailed description of the diseases of horses and the methods of keeping them healthy in his book 'Haya Ayurveda'. This book became so famous that in no time Shalihotra's name spread from one corner of India to the other. Even his name and fame reached abroad. His book *'Haya Ayurveda'* is also called *'Turangam Shastra'* or *'Shalihotra Samhita'*.

There are 1200 verses in this vast book, in which the species, breed, age etc. of the horse are described and the methods of making the horse healthy and controlling the unbridled horse are also told in an interesting way. Like an experienced guide, Shalihotra goes on telling us useful things about what precautions should be taken while buying a horse and what things should be kept in mind. In this context, Shalihotra's book *'Haya Ayurveda'* holds a different place in the Indian culture and medical world. This is an example of how developed the scientific vision was in India.

It is no less a matter of pride that even after some 2800 years of its composition, *'Haya Ayurveda'* is considered an ideal or authentic treatise on horse medicine. It has been translated into Persian, Arabic and English languages. With the passage of time, the fame of Shalihotra keeps on increasing. This shows the depth and completeness of his study.

❒

# 4

# Kanad

## Father of Indian Atomism
## (600 BC)

Kanad is counted among the oldest scientific thinkers in the world. The completeness of the new and unique theory he gave of the origin or creation of the world through 'particle' or 'atomism' still amazes. Today, when the theory of matter being made up of small indivisible atoms is prevalent and valid all over the world, the importance of Kanad increases much more. He is remembered all over the world as the 'Adi Janak' and Acharya of Atomic Theory.

Ya Kanad was one of those thinkers, for whom there was no wall or dividing line between spirituality-philosophy and science. Kanad was basically a philosopher. It is said that he was the son of Uluka Muni and was born in the 6th century BC. He lived the life of a Kanad monk, a disciple of the famous Acharya Somasharma, but he did not beg from anyone. Instead, he used to collect the grains lying on the way and used to work with them only. Because of collecting food grains, he was named Kanad.

Kanad did not have any means like today's scientists. He was able to find out the basic structure of the universe only by his intelligence. In this way he gave a theory which even today seems quite complete in itself. Because of this, Kanad is simultaneously called the greatest philosopher and scientist of India.

Kanad says that everything in the world is made of atoms. What are atoms? Considering this, they say that an atom is the smallest particle of a substance, which cannot be divided further. An atom of a substance has all the properties, characteristics etc. of that substance. But the atom cannot be seen or felt by the sense organs. These atoms often form pairs of two. Then these pairs also meet and this is how matter is created, which we can see with our eyes or touch and feel with our hands.

Kanad has divided the matter into nine elements, these are — earth, water, fire, air, sky, time, space, mind and soul. These include all the substances present in the form of solid, liquid and gas in soil, water and air. Kanad has talked about the different qualities of all substances. All substances are different in terms of colour, taste, smell, touch etc. But substances of a class also have some common properties. This is called normality. In this way, along with the generality in every substance, there is also a different specialty of its own.

Kanad also said that often when strong heat or temperature is given, there is a change in the atoms of the substance or its properties change. They refer to this chemical change of substances by the word 'pak', which means cooking. Giving an example of this, Kanad says that when a raw earthen pot is cooked on fire, not only its color but its properties also change. When raw mango is kept wrapped in a hot cloth, its color, taste etc. change. It is basically due to the interaction or change of atoms.

Like Kanad, in Greek philosophy, ideas were expressed about this atomic form or particle theory of the universe. Neusiphus and Democritus put forward their atomic theory of the creation of the world, but it did not have the perfection like Kanad. In this matter, scientists and philosophers of the world consider Kanad as the 'primordial father' of the atomic theory of the structure of the world, whose immense intellectual power we have to be fond of today.

The truth is that Kanad is like a *mayar* in the sense that reading them shows the height and perfection that India had reached in scientific principles and establishments in ancient times.

❐

# 5

# Jivak

## Great physician of ancient India (500 BC)

Jivak is also counted among the great medical scientists of India. The truth is that he look different than most of them. Due to his extraordinary abilities and qualities, his name spread so much all over India that even the biggest of kings and rich people yearned for Jivak to treat him whereas Jivak was so busy that he had to run from here to there all the time. He also used to get a lot of money from the rich people, but he did not take much money from the poor and common people. The method of treatment of Jivak was also unique and infallible, about which so many stories have come out that today we are surprised to hear them.

Jivak was born some two and a half thousand years ago in Rajgriha (Rajgir). Rajagriha was the capital of the kingdom of Magadha. Jivak was born to Shalvati, a courtesan of Rajagriha. After birth, he was thrown on a pile of mud. When Prince Abhay, the son of King Bimbasar came to know about this, he got Jivak brought up.

When Jivak came to know about his birth when he grew up, he felt very sad. He decided, "I will achieve something, so that no one laughs at me. Even the biggest people would respect me."

One day Jivak left the palace without informing the prince and reached Takshashila after a long journey. Takshashila was a big center of learning at that time. There he studied medicine deeply for many years. One day his master said, "Take this spade. Go around and come. Bring some plant which has no use in medicine."

Jivak went with the shovel. He wandered far and wide, but he did not see a single plant which was of no use. He returned and told this to the master, who said, "Go, now you are really adept in this field."

The Guru also gave some money to Jivak, so that he could return to Rajagriha on his own. But by the time he reached Ayodhya that money ran out. Jivak is worried, how will he reach home now? Then he heard that the wife of a rich man was ill. Biggest doctors tried treatment, but no one was successful. Jivak also reached there. He mixed medicines in a little ghee, after cooking a lot, cooled it and poured that ghee into the patient's nose. Within no time, the woman spit the ghee out of her mouth. By evening, she became completely healthy.

This was Jivak's first major success as a physician, due to which his fame spread far and wide. He also got a lot of money. Now he reached Rajagriha comfortably. There he came to know about the disease of King Bimbasar. He was suffering from fistula disease. Jivak cured the disease by applying medicine only once. But a strange incident happened in the case of Chandra Pradyot, the king of Avanti. It happened that for the treatment of his disease it was necessary to mix ghee in the medicine, but the king used to get irritated with ghee. Finally, Jivak found a unique way. He called the servant and asked the king to give the medicine after some time and himself went away sitting on the king's elephant. By the time the king came to know that ghee was mixed in the medicine, Jivak had reached miles away. In anger, the king asked to bring Jivak to him. The soldiers went around. But in the meantime the king's disease was cured, so he sent another soldier to call them back along with the award for Jivak.

Similarly, Jivak was widely known for surgery. A merchant in Rajgriha had severe headache. All the doctors had told him that your disease is incurable, now you will die soon. But when he went to Jivak, he performed a head surgery and made him completely fine. Similarly, the intestines of a patient were entangled. Jivak made an incision on his stomach, took out the intestines and sorted them out. Then placing them properly, stitched the skin and applied ointment. After some time the wound healed and the man's suffering also went away.

Similarly, Jivak cured Buddha's disease many times and gave him rest. Once a splinter of a rock caused severe injury to Buddha's leg. Jivak bandaged the medicine continuously, then he went to see other patients. He had thought that he would open the bandage later when he will come back at the right time. But he was late in coming. Due to the night, the gates of the city were closed and he could not enter the city.

Jivak was anguished how much trouble Mahatma Buddha must be facing due to the bandage tied on his leg. But Buddha seemed to have read Jivak's mind. He himself took off the bandage. When Jivak saw this in the morning, he was surprised and said, "Hey, how did you know about my mind?"

Buddha smiled and said, "When the mind of the patient and the doctor become one instead of remaining separate, then this happens!"

Truly, Jivak had taken the teachings of Buddha in his life. He spent his whole life in reducing the suffering of this world by giving freedom from suffering to innumerable patients. At the same time, Jivak was ideal in the sense that by reading him it can be understood how a good doctor should be alert, sensitive and deeply connected to the happiness and sorrow of others.

There can be no good doctor without service and sacrifice. That's why even after some two and a half thousand years of birth, we remember Jivak and even today we bow down before him with respect.

❐

# 6

# Charak

## Great medical scientist of ancient India (500 BC)

Charak was a medical scientist. His name is taken with great respect among the ancient medical scientists of India. His medical book *'Charak Samhita'* is still highly respected. Its importance can be understood from the fact that Patanjali wrote its commentary. Patanjali was born some two hundred years before Christ. This suggests that Charak lived several centuries before Christ.

*'Charak Samhita'* is a big book. This gives us accurate and detailed information about the medical science of ancient times. It is not difficult to guess from this that how much Indian medical science was advanced in that period and there was constant enthusiasm to make new discoveries, so that human life could be made happy and healthy.

Apart from this, we also get to know from *'Charak Samhita'* what were the ideals of the doctor of that time. While discussing the ideals of the doctor in 'Charak Samhita', it is written that he should not lie. Should be egoless. Every possible effort should be made to provide relief to the patient irrespective of his livelihood. Along with this, it has also been said that while going to see the patient, the attention of the doctor should be only on the patient; he should not pay attention to other things in the house.

It was also explained that the specialty of a good doctor is that he should not boast of his knowledge.

Charak has told many things about the anatomy of man in his book. Today our knowledge about medical science has increased a lot. Today's scientists have access to many technical means and micro instruments, due to which new discoveries are being made every day. But it is surprising to see that some two thousand years ago, when there were not even the slightest means and instruments of medicine, how Charak told so many things about human anatomy and told it correctly.

Similarly, there is wonderful information about plants in Charak's medical treatise. He mainly takes the help of plants in curing human diseases. He has classified them into different groups and described their properties and characteristics in detail. This description is so unique that even today we have to be convinced of Charak's deep studies and discoveries. Along with this, it also shows that ancient medical science was very close to nature. Unique boons of nature were used in it and that is why it can also be called Naturopathy in a sense.

Apart from this, the importance of this book of Charak is also because it revealed many interesting things about the habits, lifestyle, costumes etc. of the human beings of that time. Due to this, a correct and authentic image of the culture of that period emerges in front of our eyes.

Even today, any discussion about ancient Indian medical science is not complete without mentioning the name of Charak. He was and will remain the greatest ideal of Indian medicine. It can be known by reading Charak that what is the high ideal of a doctor? If he forgets the high ideal of service to mankind, he cannot be called a good doctor despite all his dexterity and technical skill. By remembering Charak, it seems as if the entire glorious history of Indian medical science comes before the eyes. From this, it is understood how big and unique the contribution of Charak is in Indian medical science!

❐

# 7

# Sushruta

## Great surgeon of ancient India
## (600 BC)

Sushruta was a great surgeon of India. Perhaps no one else has achieved as much fame as Sushruta in the field of surgery in ancient India. Rather, the truth is that in ancient times, India had reached a glimpse of surgery; its test and identity is from Sushruta.

The special thing is that Sushruta was as good a doctor as a teacher. With great seriousness, he explained to his students the concern of the physical structure of man, and gave them statements about surgery. Then he also used to teach surgery. He had found a unique method for this too. Earlier, he used to teach some special things, fixation of incisions on water-soaked leather bags, etc. He used to teach drawing on the body of the living being. Then after getting gradually satisfied with the talent of the students, he allowed them to perform surgery on the human body.

Sushruta performed many such surgeries, hearing about which even today we get confused. Cutting any part of the body, making incision, joining bone, plastic surgery of nose, operation of glucose and removal of stones from bladder are also such operations which are not considered special even today, but in the time of Sushruta, this was no less than a wonder.

While replacing the cut nose with a new one, Sushruta has given such a long and vivid description of every moment that it seems that we are watching a surgeon joining someone's body before our eyes. And then not only this, Sushruta also had the skill of lengthening the nose when needed and then cutting it short. It is known from this that his knowledge about the composition of the human body was amazing; his practical knowledge of surgery was also amazing. In this matter, not only in his era, but for many eras to come, he was considered a Master of many masters in this field. Behind this, of course, was the expertise of his practical experiences, due to which he gave unimaginable heights to surgery.

Similarly, Sushruta also used to perform stomach surgery. He found a unique way to reconnect the intestines when they were injured. He brought the ends of the intestines close to each other and released large ants there. These ants used to cut the ends of the intestines and hold them tightly. Then Sushruta used to cut the body of the ants. This prevented the ants from harming the body and the intestines were firmly attached, as if tied with strong hooks. Instead, if the intestines are tied with a thread or something, they shrink. For this reason, Sushruta devised this unique method which is still used in some places in surgery.

Apart from this, Sushruta also described in detail how the seasons affect the human body and what precautions should be taken or which vegetables, etc. should be used in which season. Sushruta has also given an interesting description of the effect of air coming from different directions on the human body. Sushruta has also divided the flora and fauna into different categories on the basis of their common qualities.

It is a proof of Sushruta's study that most of his sayings seem to be correct even today. Some of his things may prove to be incomplete or wrong today, but this much goes to show that despite very limited and very modest equipment, he had immense talent. He took the work of instruments not only with instruments, but also with the mind. The knowledge he gained from this and the unique discoveries he made, will continue to inspire humans for centuries to come.

❐

# 8

# Aryabhatta

## India's great mathematician and scholar (476 AD)

Aryabhatta is counted among the great scholars of ancient India. Not only was he a great mathematician, he also invented his own unique method of measuring time. Similarly, he gave a logical scientific explanation to the lunar eclipse by refuting many myths about it. Due to this many people turned against Aryabhatta. But Aryabhatta, engaged in the search for scientific truth, did not care at all and said only what he thought was right. This is the reason why he is counted among the great scientists and mathematicians of ancient India.

Aryabhatta was born about one and a half thousand years ago. There is a difference of opinion regarding his place of birth. Some people say that he was born in Kusumpur, while some other scholars consider his birthplace as Pataliputra.

Looking at Aryabhatta's time, his ideas seem quite revolutionary. He was a true thinker, logician and scientist and was far ahead of other scientists of his time. Aryabhatta's thoughts and principles are in the texts written by him. He composed a total of three books, *'Aryabhatiya'*, *'Dava-Deshika Sutra'* and *'Aryashta Shat'*. In these there are ten shlokas in Arya verses in *'Aryabhatiya'*. In *'Dash-Deshika Sutra'* he has told about his calculation system. There are 108 verses in the third book *'Aryashta Shat'*, in which mathematics, geography and the method of measuring time are described.

Aryabhatta was as great a mathematician and astrologer as he was also a great scientist. Till now it was said about the lunar eclipse that due to the eclipse of Rahu, the moon gets eclipsed. But Aryabhatta refused to accept it. Explaining the lunar eclipse in a very logical way, he said that due to the coming of the Earth between the Sun and the Moon, the light of the Sun could not reach the Moon. That's why lunar eclipse happens. One and a half thousand years ago, he had come to know this scientific truth and told it with great courage. It can be said that his explanation of lunar eclipse was completely scientific and it shows that in ancient times India was really world leader in scientific research.

Aryabhatta knew very well that the moon does not have its own light. It shines only by the light of the Sun. Similarly, it is because of the Sun that there are day and night on the earth and the seasons keep on changing; this truth was also known by him from his scientific study of space and he also expressed it in a very effective way.

It can be said, in this matter Aryabhatta was far ahead of his time. At a time when we did not have much means to study the position of the planets, etc. and had to see and verify everything with our own eyes, Aryabhatta's extremely scientific establishments amazed and marvelled.

It is surprising that the scholars who worked in this field after Aryabhatta preferred to go back instead of taking these scientific establishments forward. Not only this, on the contrary, they condemned Aryabhatta. Varahamihir and Brahmagupt, who were born about a hundred years after Aryabhatta, bitterly criticized and condemned Aryabhatta's theory of lunar eclipse. They said that Aryabhatta, by his new setting of lunar eclipse, insulted Indian tradition and myths.

The truth is that the pandas, priests were angry with Aryabhatta's statements about the lunar eclipse. That's why even known people like Varahamihir and Brahmagupt could not dare to speak the truth after being terrorized by them. Aryabhatta was a true truth-seeking scientist, who only took the foundation of truth and did not care about pandas and priests.

But this courage proves Aryabhatta to be a great scientist. Today we know that Aryabhatta was right and he was thinking far ahead of the scholars who were born years later. This increases our respect for this great truth-seeking scientist.

❒

# 9

# Khan

## Incredible woman scientist of ancient India (500 AD)

Women also contributed to the development of Indian science during the ancient period, even though their number was not very large. Khan was one of those brilliant women scientists. Unfortunately, today we do not have much information about Khan's life, but today we get very beautiful quotes composed by her, which give an introduction to her talent. Most of Khan's aphorisms are about agriculture and they are true on the soil of Bengal. From this, it was speculated that she might have been from Bengal. Khan probably existed in the 6th century.

Most of Khaṇ's aphorisms are about agriculture and they are so accurate and authentic that even today a lot can be learned from them. For example, they say that the best farming is that in which family members do farming together. The crop gets half-incomplete from the farming done by others. Similarly, he said many important things about the rain. When it is good to rain and when it is not, she says that even the king has to beg if it rains in Agrahayana. Similarly, she says that if there is a lot of rain on the ninth day of the Krishna Paksha of Ashadh, then the stork will have to walk on the bottom of the sea; that means there will be severe drought. But if there is a light drizzle on this day, it will rain so much throughout the year that the fish will settle on the tops of the mountains.

Khan has also said many useful things about plowing the land and sowing crops. She says that the land should be plowed ten times for radish, so that the land becomes soft like mustard. But there is absolutely no need for plowing for betel. Khan did not consider it good to plow on the day of full moon or new moon. Her point was to say that it causes unrest in the house; it can even lead to the apocalypse.

Khan says that paddy should be sown in Ashadh and not in Sawan or Bhadon. Peas should be sown in Ashwin Kartik and mustard should be sown at the end of autumn. Her advice to the farmers is that they should leave the game of backgammon and sow turmeric in Vaishakh and Jeth and weed the soil in Ashadh and Sawan, so that it becomes fully cultivable.

Khan's style of speaking is unique and there is a new pose in it, due to which her proverbs became the jewels of the hearts of the people. Even today people mention her in every conversation. Khan's sense of humor is also reflected in these sayings. For example, at one place she says that by planting betel leaves in Sawan, the yield will be so high that even Ravana cannot chew them!

Obviously, in Khan's words, there is not only useful knowledge of agriculture, but there is also a lesson of deep understanding, poetic art and hard work, behind which somewhere the imagination of an ideal farmer's life is also hidden. That's why Khan's words are still fondly remembered today.

❐

# 10

# Varahamihir

## Master of Astronomy
## (499 AD)

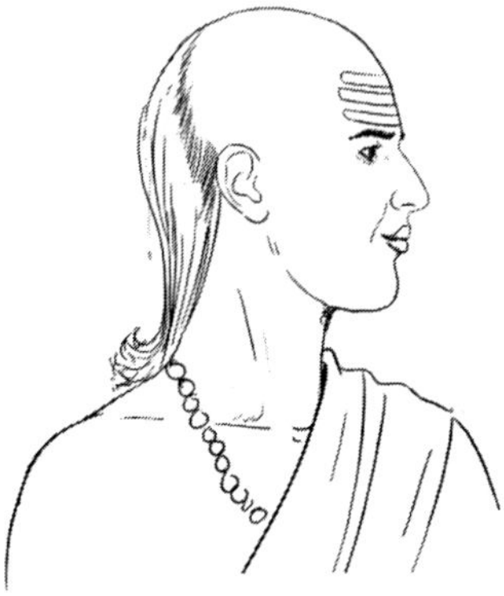

Varahamihir was a great astronomer of ancient India, whose talent and knowledge are always respected. Along with other scholars of astronomy, we are also indebted to Varahamihir for the information we have about mathematical astrology and fruitful astrology today.

Varahamihir was born at the end of the fifth century in the city of Ujjayini. His father's name was Adityadas. Varahamihir was very devoted and studious. Soon the fame of his scholarship spread everywhere. He put forward his principles related to astronomy, which shows his deep understanding.

Varahamihir clearly stated that the earth is spherical. But in the sphere we have found some place high and some low. So is there any place on earth high and any low? Varahamihir answers this question very beautifully. He used to say that there is neither high nor low among the people living on the Earth. Giving the example of the branches of the Kadamba tree, he says that on any branch of the Kadamba tree, flowers bloom everywhere. We seem to have them up and down, but if we look in the context of the branch, then the truth is that every flower has blossomed on the top of the branch. Exactly the same is the condition of the living beings on the Earth. They are all above the Earth and they all have their own sky, so they are not high and low, but on the same plane.

This statement of Varahamihir is completely correct. But he also made a big mistake regarding the motions of the earth and other planets. Actually Varahamihir considered the earth to be stable. He said that the earth is stable and the sun, moon and other planets revolve around it. Varahamihir could not accept that the earth has motion or that it rotates. He had a very strange argument that if the earth were to rotate, then a bird that has flown west would not be able to return to its nest immediately. He could not understand that as the earth rotates, the bird bound by its gravity also rotates simultaneously and its position with respect to the earth remains the same or constant.

A major basis of Varahmihir's fame is his famous book '*Panchsiddhanta*'. This is a very interesting and great book of Indian astronomy. In this book, Varahamihir has given great scholarly information about the five major theories of astronomy of that time: Polish, Romak, Vasistha, Surya and Pitamah. Among these, the Surya Siddhanta has got the most recognition. Varahamihir modified Aryabhatta's ideas about Surya Siddhanta and gave it a new form.

One specialty of Varahamihir was that he was very educated. The principles of astronomy that he has discussed, namely Polish and Romak, can be said to be based on the astronomical principles of Alexandria and Rome. Thus there was clearly Greek influence on Varahamihir. At one place, he has also praised the fact that the Greeks may have other faults, but they are well versed in science.

Apart from "Panchsiddhanta", there is a major work of Varahamihir — 'Brihad Samhita'. In one of its sections, he has written very useful and useful things about farming. He has also considered the importance of manure for planting good fruits and flowers. Along with this, Varahamihir has written many interesting things about how to plant plants and what precautions should be taken in it. He also said that a prediction of the upcoming drought or rain can also be inferred if we look at the plants carefully.

We do not like all the words of Varahamihir today. Even Aryabhatta, who was born a hundred years before him, had established the earth to revolve continuously on its keel. Varahamihir denied this. But today we know that Aryabhatta, not Varahamihir, was right and Varahamihir took his establishments backwards instead of taking them forward. Yet Varahamihir was certainly a scholar. He had a unique erudition with a deep understanding of astronomy, from which a lot can be learned even today.

❐

# 11

# Brahmagupta

## Great master of Algebra
## (598 AD)

Brahmagupta is counted among the great mathematicians of India. Especially, the mathematician Brahmagupta was the one who gave such clear, logical and correct information about zero for the first time. India's biggest contribution to the world's knowledge and science is the discovery of zero. Brahmagupt was among the great mathematicians who discovered this zero.

Brahmagupta was born at the end of the sixth century in the city of Bhillamal near Multan. His father's name was Jishnu. By the time Brahmagupta was born, the Gupta Empire had declined. Therefore, there was no atmosphere of enthusiasm as before in the field of knowledge-science and culture. But Brahmagupta not only seriously read the books of eminent scholars of astronomy and mathematics, but also added a lot of new and valuable things to this stream of knowledge-science on his own behalf. The *'Brahmasphuta-siddhanta'* is the most famous of the texts written by Brahmagupta. In this book, he has given very interesting and useful information about Algebra, Arithmetic, Geometry and Astronomy. Apart from the very complete concept of zero, Brahmagupta also did such a huge and remarkable work in the field of algebra for the first time, which is enough to earn him the status of a top Indian Mathematician.

Brahmagupta's information about zero surprises us the most today. He has written about this in the '*Kuttakadhyaya*' of his treatise '*Brahmasphuta-siddhanta*', which contains information about algebra. Brahmagupta has clearly said that subtraction of zero from any negative number results in a loss. When zero is subtracted from a positive number, we get a positive number only, whereas if zero is subtracted from zero, we get zero only.

Similarly, he said that if zero is multiplied by any negative or positive number, then the result is zero. Even if zero is multiplied by zero, the result is zero. But if a number is divided by zero, then the result is not this, but the result becomes infinite. Similarly, he said another thing that if zero is divided by zero, then the result is not zero, but an undetermined or indefinite number is found in the result. No less exciting is the fact that many centuries after Brahmagupta's principles, our knowledge and discoveries about mathematics today justify them.

The knowledge and scholarship of Algebra is immense. The rules he gave to solve simple and two degree equations still amaze us. The special thing is that this extraordinary knowledge of algebra was used by Brahmagupta in mathematics, astrology, etc. and thus created a unique revolution in this field. Brahmagupta himself knew his talent and its importance in the field of algebra, due to which he was considered the top mathematician of his time.

At one place, he has written in a very interesting and poetic way, "Just as the light of the sun dims the stars, in the same way a learned scholar in algebra dulls the brilliance of other astronomers in the assembly."

Like Aryabhatta and Varahamihir, Brahmagupta also knew very well that the earth is round in shape. In his book, he has also written about this in a very impressive way. Brahmagupta refused to accept the fact written in many ancient texts and Puranas that the earth is flat. He also did not believe that the earth was hollow from inside like a stone.

Brahmagupta said that if we study the positions of the stars at different places and their rising and setting, it proves itself that the earth is spherical. All the calculations of Astronomy are proved correct on this basis.

Obviously, like Aryabhatta and Varahamihir, Brahmagupta also seems to be logically advancing an important astronomical idea here. But Brahmagupta had a big limitation too. Like Varahamihir, he also strongly criticized Aryabhatta's idea that the earth revolves on its axis. Rather, for this reason, Brahmagupta condemned Aryabhatta in harsh words by calling him anti-tradition. He also repeats Varahamihir's argument that if the earth were to rotate, birds that had flown from their nests would never return to their homes. But today we know that this discovery of Brahmagupta is incomplete and wrong. Aryabhatta, who was born about 125 years before him, was able to think far ahead of him in this matter.

Instead of taking Aryabhatta's ideas forward, Brahmagupta tried to reverse them. May be behind this, there was a fear of the prominent pundits or astrologers, etc. of that time, because they used to do all the calculations considering the Earth as stable and the Sun as dynamic. Prominent historian and world traveler Al-Biruni, who came to India in those days, also believes that perhaps he did not believe in what Brahmagupta said. Fearing the Brahmins and astrologers of his time, he did not tell the truth.

Nevertheless, there can be no doubt that Brahmagupta was the great mathematician of India. His importance was acknowledged not only in India, but all over the world. Brahmagupta's famous treatise *'Brahmasphuta-siddhanta'* was called *'Sindh Hind'* in Arabic and by reading it, people of Arab had learned many new things about astronomy.

❐

# 12

# Vagbhata

## Great Physician of Ancient India (600 AD)

Among ancient Indian physicians, like Atreya and Sushruta, the name of Vagbhata is also taken with great respect. At some places, Atreya, Sushruta and Vagbhata are also mentioned as a large trinity. The truth is that Vagbhata has a big hand in bringing Indian medical science to perfection and making it more and more useful and meaningful for humans. Without them ancient medicine and its heights cannot be estimated.

Vagbhata was born in the country of Sindh at the end of the sixth century. His father's name was Singhgupta. Vagbhata has been interested in medical science since childhood. His guru was the Buddhist teacher Avalokita. It was under his guidance that Vagbhata began a serious study of ancient medical texts and within a few years he was counted among the accomplished and well-versed scholars of this field. Vagbhata was a Vedic Brahmin by birth. But later on he was influenced by Buddhism and the teachings of Mahatma Buddha. That's why there is praise of Mahatma Buddha at many places in his book *'Ashtanga Sangraha'*.

His famous books, *'Ashtanga Sangraha'* and *'Ashtang Hriday Samhita',* made Vagbhata's fame indestructible.

Some people say that Vagbhata is not one but two, i.e. the author of *'Ashtanga Hriday Samhita'* was someone else. But this does not seem to be the case with the exact same names of both the texts. Then, in the *'Ashtang Hridaya Samhita'*, the verses of the *Ashtanga Samhita* are quoted liberally and without naming the author; it also seems that Vagbhata is not two, but one. The reason for some difference in the style of both the texts seems to be that *'Ashtanga Sangraha'* is an early work of Vagbhata, while later he expressed his thoughts with more maturity and completeness in *'Ashtanga Hridaya Samhita..*

But whatever may be the reason, Vagbhata's *'Astanga Sangraha'* book has been more discussed. Divided into six sections, this book has a total of 150 chapters. There is hardly any aspect related to body and health, which has escaped Vagbhata's keen eye. Not only the description and interpretation of diseases, etc. in the book, the classification of subjects is also very scientific.

In the first section, there is more general discussion about the awareness of life and health. There are many useful things that come in handy in everyday life. How to get long life; how to teach medical science to the students; what are the merits or demerits of different types of vegetables; how to detect poisons and diseases etc. and how to avoid them; how to do gargling; the treatment of eye diseases by cold application, etc. are described in a very detailed and interesting way in this section.

In the second section, scientific information about human anatomy has been given in great detail. The third section deals with diabetes, boils and skin diseases. While Vagbhata explains in detail about the symptoms of diseases, he also gives complete information about their diagnosis. The fourth section deals with defecation and vomiting, while the fifth and sixth sections contain information about proper child rearing, etc.

Like *'Ashtanga Sangraha'*, Vagbhata's book *'Ashtang Hridaya Samhita'* is also divided into six sections and there are 120 chapters in total. This book quoted in detail the opinions of famous medical scientists like Vagbhata, Dhanvantari, Charak, Sushruta, along with the methods of staying healthy, giving complete information about Ayurveda in an interesting style. In particular, he has explained the principles of medical science in a very easy way.

The importance of Vagbhata can be understood from the fact that Sharangadhar, Chakrapani Dutt and Bhavmishra, who came after him, have mentioned his words with great respect. The truth is that Vagbhata was also among the great scientists who gave a strong foundation to ancient Indian medical science, whose importance is increasing day by day.

❐

# 13

# Madhavkar

## Ancient physician of India
## (900 AD)

Madhavkar also has an important place in ancient Indian medicine. Madhavkar's name was also Madhavacharya or Vidyaranya. Madhavkar's essential characteristic was that he had a lot of expertise and proficiency in the diagnosis of disease, that is why the famous book 'Rugvinishchhaya' composed by him is also known as 'Madhav-'Nidan' or 'Nidan'.

Madhavkar was born at a place called Kishkindha in South India, which is also known today as Golconda. Madhavkar also had a brother Sayana, who wrote a beautiful commentary on the Rigveda. Madhavkar is said to have been a minister and guide of the mighty Vijayanagara kingdom in South India. He also wrote books on astronomy, etc. In his old age, he became a monk and started creating a wave of renaissance in the society and engaged in social reform.

The biggest feature of Madhavkar's medicine is that it is based more on the spirit of public welfare than on medical ostentation or display of scholarship. Madhavkar, like a great doctor, gives detailed information about various diseases, their symptoms and the methods to get rid of them, by telling people the basic mantra to stay healthy or protect their health.

It is no less surprising that where other medical scientists go ahead with a little information about the diagnosis of diseases, the basic goal of Madhavkar and his book is to give people information about disease diagnosis in simple language. Broadly speaking, it is an ideal doctor warning people to be careful about their health.

There is also a special thing that if compared with the texts or medical methods of Charaka or Sushruta, the medical science of Madhavkar's time would definitely be considered more advanced. The reason is that along with including good parts and features of earlier texts, continuous experiments, new discoveries and achievements in the field of medical science have also been included. Thus the complexity is relatively less and the quality of a doctor directly addressing people is more prominent.

If you take into account Madhavkar's life-time, it can be clearly said that he was born after Vagbhata and before Dradhaval and Vrind. This is the reason why Vagbhata mentions Charak and Sushruta, but not Madhavkar. Similarly, there is no discussion of Dradhaval and Vrind in Madhavkar's texts. From this point of view, it can be inferred that Madhavkar might have lived in the ninth or tenth century.

Scholars like Vijayrakshit and Srikanthadatta wrote commentaries on Madhavkar's book. This also shows their historical importance in Indian medicine.

Researchers of Indian medical science even today do not forget to mention this unique saint and medical scientist with respect due to the originality of thinking and many great features.

❒

# 14

# Dradhbal

## Who carried forward the work of Charak (900 AD)

Among the ancient scientists of India, the name of Kashmiri scientist Dradhbal is also mentioned with respect. Dradhbal's study of medicine is unique. He used this immense knowledge and study and revised *'Charak Samhita'* according to his time and its needs.

Dradhbal was a very brilliant and talented scientist. His father's name was Kapibal. Dradhbal was born in Panchnadpur in the $9^{th}$ century AD. This place is about seven miles away from Srinagar. The confluence of five rivers namely Vitasta, Indus, Kshirabhavani, Trigama and Anakara is very close to this place. That's why it was called Panchnadpur. From childhood, Dradhbal's proclivity was towards the study of ancient texts of medicine, etc. especially *'Charak Samhita',* which was his favourite book.

Dradhbal was upset to see that the ancient form of *'Charak Samhita'* is no longer available and many important parts of it have been completely destroyed. Apart from this, one of the reasons for his concern was that the form in which the book *'Charak Samhita'* was available, despite its extraordinary historical importance, seemed somewhat outdated according to that time. Some things which could have been more useful in terms of the health of the common people were dealt with briefly and many unnecessary things were discussed in a confusing manner, with much unnecessary detail. That is why, Dradhbal felt the need of editing *'Charak Samhita'*.

Finally, after much deliberation, Dradhbal decided to edit *'Charak Samhita'*. But it was not an easy task. For this, he thoroughly researched all the new and old texts of medical information and collected useful things from them according to his time. He also got many ancient rare books of medical science, which he read word for word and meditated on it thoroughly. Then he got involved in the very serious and responsible work of editing *'Charak Samhita'*.

The challenge in front of Dradhbal was giving information about diseases, etc. to the human beings of his time, treatment of diseases and protection of their health by proper medicines. In this context, he had to reduce the unnecessary expansion of *Charaka Samhita* at many places. The essential and useful things for the common people were dealt with in brief there; Dradhbal wrote interestingly giving them a lot of detail. Apart from this, in order to make *'Charak Samhita'* a complete medical book, he took necessary material from other authentic texts of medical science and added it to *'Charak Samhita'* and made it a more useful and complete book.

Chakrapani Dutt later commented on the book *'Charak Samhita'* edited by Dradhbal. He called this treatise *'Kashmir Path'*, as it was a kind of Kashmiri version of Indian medical science and *'Charaka Samhita'*. Of course, there was also a deep impression of Dradhbal's own talent and thinker personality.

Dradhbal was completely successful in his endeavour. The truth is that Dradhbal's contribution in protecting *'Charak Samhita'* from the ravages of time and giving it perfection is a thing of historical importance. *'Charak Samhita'* in the form available to us today, is the book edited by Dradhbal. In this context, the importance of this exceptionally talented Kashmiri scientist increases even more among the ancient Indian scientists.

❒

# 15

# Nagarjuna

## The great chemist of India
## (931 AD)

Nagarjuna is called the great alchemist of India. There have been many such anecdotes about him that he was friendly with the gods and used to come to earth when they called. There are also many anecdotes about his immense achievements and it is said that he could create any metal he wanted by mixing metals together or by chemical action. In this regard, more anecdotes are associated with Nagarjuna than with any other Indian scientist. It is definitely known from these anecdotes that Nagarjuna was a wonderful alchemist and he had amazing perfection in making different compounds of metals through chemical reactions and in this way, giving new forms to metals.

As such, we do not get much information about Nagarjuna's life today. He was born in 931AD in Dehak district near Somnath in Gujarat and was extremely brilliant. Because of his amazing talent, people considered him a miracle child. In many important texts, astonishing things are read about him. Famous traveler Al-Biruni has mentioned Nagarjuna with great respect and has written that he was perfect in the alchemy of chemicals.

Al-Biruni has also mentioned Nagarjuna's famous book *'Ras-Ratnakar'* and said that we get the essence of all the knowledge-science that was there till now in Nagarjuna's book *'Ras-Ratnakar'*. In other books written by Nagarjuna, *'Kakshaput Tantra'*, *'Arogya Manjari'*, '*Yogsar*' and '*Yogshatak*' are also discussed, but his most famous and immortal book is *'Ras-Ratnakar'*. Apart from this, another important work of Nagarjuna is editing *'Sushruta Samhita'*. He added very important material obtained from the research of the changed times in '*Sushruta Samhita*'. The form of *'Sushruta Samhita'* that we get today is the modified form by Nagarjuna. This shows that not only in his own time, but also in later times, Nagarjuna's scholarship received the same fame and people had deep respect for him.

The things written in *'Ras-Ratnakar'* attracted not only the scholars but also the common people. In this, Nagarjuna's language is so attractive and poetic that it captivates everyone. He knew how to present even the smallest matter of knowledge in an enticing manner. A sample of Nagarjuna's language is, "How wonderful it is that vermilion (red mercuric Sulphide) imparts to silver the luster of gold like saffron after being exposed several times in vegetable acids and sheep's milk." Similarly, at one place, he tells that by mixing some special chemicals in silver, they convert it into a substance weighing seven times its weight, whose brightness is like that of the Sun.

Nagarjuna also had expertise in making different compounds of mercury, but for this he had to do a long meditation. At one place he writes that he worshiped Goddess Yakshini for about twelve years for the welfare of the people. Then he heard a divine voice, "Oh great sage! Whatever you want, I will give you everything." At this Nagarjuna prayed, "O Devi, if you are pleased with me, bestow on me the rare knowledge of making compounds of mercury."

Nagarjuna also told many such amazing things about mercury, which astonish us even today. Many diseases can be cured by mercury and when consumed in the right way, man can get immense strength, power and energy. Nagarjuna has given information about this very interestingly.

The knowledge that Nagarjuna acquired through his life-long research was preserved by the generations to come. He has a great contribution in the development of Indian knowledge-science and culture. Even after Nagarjuna, there were alchemists like Vrinda and Chakrapani, who took his work further. But he also repeatedly refers to Nagarjuna as 'the great master of alchemical art'. We find excerpts from many books written by Nagarjuna in the works of Vrinda and Chakrapani.

All of Nagarjuna's writings may not be available today, but whatever we have today, our respect for this great chemist of ancient times continues to grow.

❐

# 16

# Vrind

## Ancient chemists of India (1000 AD)

Vrind is also discussed among the ancient scientists of India. Vrind was a prominent and extraordinary chemist who carried forward Nagarjuna's work in the field of alchemy. He played an important role in the development of chemistry in India.

Much information about Vrind's life is not available to us today. Yes, it can be inferred that he was born a thousand years ago. In this context, he was born after the famous saint and scientist Madhavkar and before Chakrapani Dutt. The name of Vrind's main work is *'Siddha Yoga'*, in which there is a lot of material related to medical chemistry. In this context, the name of Vrind cannot be forgotten in the history of medicine.

In his book *'Siddha Yoga'*, Vrind, along with a detailed description of the chemicals that help in keeping man healthy, has also described the measures by which man can avoid diseases and other physical disorders. It also describes in detail the medicines used in various diseases. Vrind has given a step-by-step description of how to prepare metal compounds. Similarly, how to make iron ash, Vrind has explained it very clearly. The special thing is that Vrind has discussed many such things, which are used in everyday life. For example, the use of mercury is very useful in the medicine used to kill lice.

Vrind has also discussed this. By the time of Vrinda, the use of mercury and sulphur in medicines had become very common. This thing becomes clear after reading about his book *'Rasamrit Churna'*.

Overall, Vrinda was a remarkable alchemist who carried forward the tradition of Nagarjuna. One of the special features of his treatise *'Siddha Yoga'* is that in this Vrind has freely quoted the ideas of eminent scientists Charak, Sushruta, Nagarjuna, Vagbhata and Madhavkar before him and literally took a lot of material from their texts. Thus Vrind's treatise *'Siddha Yoga'* contains in itself many useful arrays of the history of India's continuously developing chemistry. For this reason, the name of Vrind automatically became important among the ancient scientists of India.

❐

# 17

# Bhaskaracharya

## Mathematician of extraordinary intelligence (1114 AD)

Bhaskaracharya was also among the ancient mathematicians of India, whose extraordinary understanding and genius still amazes us. Especially in Algebra, he was a proven teacher. The unique formulas he gave to solve complex mathematical problems are still in use today. The pinnacle to which he took his mathematical discoveries in the twelfth century continues to astonish mathematicians all over the world. At that time hardly anywhere in the world the knowledge of mathematics had reached the height where Bhaskaracharya had reached.

Bhaskar was born in 1114 AD at Vijjadavid, a place in Maharashtra. His father's name was Maheshwar. Maheshwar himself was a scholar of mathematics. He himself taught mathematics to Bhaskar. Bhaskar not only learned everything quickly, but his talent increased in the direction of finding new mathematical formulas. At the age of 36, Bhaskar had composed his great book of mathematics *'Siddhant Shiromani'*.

*'Siddhant Shiromani'* is a big book, which has four parts — Patiganit or Lilavati, Vijganit, Grah Ganitadhyay and Goladhyay.

In this, in the first part Patiganit or Lilavati, many interesting and new things have been told about arithmetic. It is said that Lilavati was Bhaskar's daughter, whom he used to teach mathematics very interestingly. Therefore, he named this part of the book after the name of his daughter Lilavati.

Other parts of this book also include Algebra, which contains a very detailed study of the principles of algebra. Graha-Ganitadhyaya describes the motions of planets, etc., while Goladhyaya, written in a very interesting style, contains formulas for calculations related to circles, etc.

Lilavati, the first part of Bhaskar's book, is very interesting and important from many points of view. In this, the rules of mathematics, etc. which Aryabhatt, Brahmagupta, etc. told in their works, have been put forward in an easy to understand manner. The structure of the questions is also very funny, in which there is humour like a story. For example, a mathematics question given in Lilavati reads, "In a group of swans, a pair of swans kept playing on the water. The pair observed that tired of changing directions seven times half of the square root of the total group, the swans are walking towards the shore. Dear girl, tell me, how many swans were there in the group?"

Similarly, in the second part of Vijganit, there is information about the methods of Algebra and those principles, due to which big calculations are done in a pinch. The biggest feature of this part is Bhaskaracharya's information about zero. Bhaskar rightly tells us about zero in the twelfth century. They know that adding or removing zero from a number makes no difference, but multiplying a number by zero gives the product zero. Similarly, dividing a number by zero gives infinity. Bhaskar puts this point in front very skillfully.

In the third part of the book, in the Grahaganita chapter, there is a detailed description of astronomy i.e. the motions of planets, etc. Bhaskar has considered air as the reason for the movements of the planets. Today we do not consider this astronomical theory of Bhaskar more important. Bhaskar has also analysed the movement of the Sun regarding the length of the day. The relation of circumference, diameter, etc. of a circle has been explained in the fourth part of the book, Goladhyay. Very interesting things have also been said about the mutual relation of shapes like circle, triangle, etc.

Realising the importance of Bhaskar's book, the Mughal emperor Akbar got the first part of this book 'Lilavati' translated into Persian. This translation was done by Abul Fazl in 1587. Since then, the fame of this unique book of Bhaskar has not reduced in the world, but keeps growing unabatedly.

❐

# 18

# Bhoj Narhari

## The great ship specialist of ancient India (1200 AD)

The name of Bhoj Narhari is not very well known. But this does not diminish the importance of his work. Bhoj Narhari was an expert in shipbuilding. Not only is his extensive study in this field, but also new discoveries and deep understanding that is astonishing.

Bhoj Narhari was born around the twelfth century. He has written in his book that a feast has taken place even before him. Perhaps he was referring to Raja Bhoj in the eleventh century, who was a successful king as well as a good writer.

The name of Bhoj Narhari's unique treatise on the ship, its structure and different characteristics is *'Yukti Kalpataru'*. In this book, along with interesting descriptions of different types of ships, he also tells us about their names, sizes and different types of decorations.

In 'Yukti Kalpataru', the variety of different types of ships, their sizes, the wood used to make them and the methods of construction are written with in-depth detail and authority. After reading it, there is no doubt that in ancient times, India has been a very advanced country regarding ship art and sea voyages. The traders here used to send their goods out through the sea and also get them ordered. Apart from this, ships were also made for traveling and enjoying sea travel.

Even warships had evolved at that time and their design was different.

Bhoj Narhari in his book has broadly described two categories of ships. The first category describes ships used for general river travel. It has been kept in the general category. However, further ten types have been made regarding the size, etc. of the vessels of general category. Among these, the smallest vessel 'Kshudra' is sixteen cubits long, while the largest 'Manthar' is one hundred and twenty cubits long. According to Bhoj's description, their width and height also increase in the same proportion.

Bhoj Narhari has created two main categories of sea vessels – long and advanced. There are further subtypes in both of these categories. The smallest of the long-range ships is the Galgika, which is thirty-two cubits long and the largest 'Vegini', which is seventy-six cubits long. Similarly, the ships of the advanced region range from the length of thirty-two cubits to the length of ninety-six cubits. The smallest of these is 'Urdh' and the largest is 'Manthar'.

Bhoj Narhari also said that such ships should be used to carry royal treasures and horses and women, whose main chambers are end to end. These were called the Golden Temple. Similarly, the middle temple and front temple were also water vessels. Bhoj Narhari has also told many useful things about the wood used to make these ships. Bhoj Narhari's description about the colour and decoration of the ships is also very interesting, due to which not only his knowledge but also art and refined aesthetic sense is also revealed.

The specialty of Bhoj Narhari is that in his treatise he has discussed almost every aspect of shipbuilding art in detail. There is hardly anything of importance relating to the shipwreck that has been missed by him. India was not only very advanced in the matter of ships in ancient times, it was a world leader. This is known by reading Bhoj Narhari.

Marco Polo has also enthusiastically described this wonderful skill and scientific knowledge of India. But none of the texts had such complete and authoritative information about ships. In this context, the importance of Bhoj Narhari and his book increases much more. It really fills us with joy today to remember Bhoj Narhari as a special expert of ancient knowledge.

❐

# 19

# Bhavmishra

## Medieval medical science in India (Circa 1600 AD)

Bhavmishra is considered to be an exceptionally talented physician among the medieval medical scientists of India. He gave new life to Indian medical science and its principles through his famous book '*Bhavprakash*' and his unique medical principles.

It is commonly believed that Indian science was very advanced in ancient times and by the time it came to the medieval period, it had become decadent. Generally this is not wrong. But there have also been extraordinary medical scientists like Bhavmishra in the Middle Ages, who hoisted the flag of the achievements of Indian Ayurveda all around.

Bhavmishra was born in Banaras in the sixteenth century. His father's name was Latka Mishra Bhav Mishra not only studied all the ancient texts of medical science seriously, but also learned the latest methods of medical science in practice and achieved perfection in them. In no time, the fame of Bhavmishra's name spread everywhere. He was considered the most qualified and popular doctor of his time, whose joint doctor was second to none in the whole of India.

Bhavmitra included the essence of his studies, knowledge and experiences of medical science in his famous book 'Bhavprakash'.

In this book, Bhavmishra has told many useful things about human anatomy, origin and development of Indian medical science, diet and diseases of children etc. Bhavmishra's style is very interesting and beautiful and he goes ahead explaining his point very clearly.

In his book, Bhavmishra has inspired the thoughts of his former medical scientists at many places, and has also written down his experiences and thoughts in simple language. Along with Indian medicines, he has also mentioned the medicines of other countries. This shows that by the time of Bhavmishra, the influence of the medical system of other countries was also being seen here.

Another special thing was that along with the arrival of foreigners, many types of diseases also came in India. Among these, the name of one disease was Firang Rog. Bhavmishra has mentioned three stages of this disease. According to him, the disease can be treated in the first stage, but it is difficult to avoid it in the second and third stage.

Bhavmishra did a great service to Indian medical science by giving a book named '*Bhavprakash*' because it shows the continuous development of Indian medical science. Along with this, many ancient knowledge and information about medicines, etc. had also disappeared. Through '*Bhavprakash*' we get to know these healing methods again. And thus it became a rare coincidence of revival of ancient Indian medical knowledge. In this sense, the name and work of Bhavmishra in Indian medical science is unforgettable.

❐

# 20

# Emperor Jahangir

## A unique ornithologist and astronomer (1569–1627)

The famous ornithologists of India also include the name of a great historical figure, the Mughal Emperor Jahangir. Jahangir had to fight many wars. The preoccupations of governance were in their place. Despite this, his love for birds was so much that he knew not only the form, shape, etc. of birds, but also the minute details about their nature, habits and reproduction. Despite being an emperor, he spent much of his life in bird watching. Pictures of birds were also made by famous painters. There is a lot of historical evidence of to show how deep his study was in this regard.

Born on September 9, 1569, Jahangir's love for nature is well known. From childhood, he was fascinated by the beautiful images of nature. Even when he grew up, he did not lose his passion. Yes, bird-love was added to it, which later turned into such a scientific study that Jahangir is counted among the world's most famous ornithologists. Wherever Jahangir went, he studied the beautiful birds there and collected all the information about them in detail.

He himself also had a small zoo, which made it easier for him to observe birds. To find out about the nature or habits of the birds, he had to sit for hours in the zoo and take notes of the smallest things. Then he would reach in to some conclusion and he would get real happiness and satisfaction. His conclusions and details seem so correct and important even today that the famous ornithologist Salim Ali had to say with surprise, "The memoirs of Emperor Jahangir are the encyclopedia of natural science of India at that time."

Jahangir has described the nature of birds in such an interesting way that even today it creates interest in us to go closer to the world of birds. For example, he told that in stork pairs, both the male and the female incubate the eggs alternately. Jahangir has also described in a very interesting way how children come out of these eggs and how both male and female storks take care of them together. Even today these things are of great use in terms of scientific study and their authenticity is accepted by all.

A major contribution of Jahangir in the field of bird-watching is that he called the greatest painters of his time and asked them to make pictures of birds. The painters were rewarded and these paintings were preserved. On the basis of these pictures, we came to know new things about many birds. It was also known about such birds which were there in the time of Jahangir, but not today. Jahangir got their pictures made by famous painters of his time. When one such picture passed through the eyes of ornithologists, they were astonished. They accepted with great respect the importance of Jahangir's bird-watching and bird-love.

Similarly, Jahangir's observations, conclusions and records as an astronomer are today like historical documents. Not only did he keep the details of lunar eclipse, solar eclipse, etc., as well as many of his observations about comets are used today as historical evidence.

Jahangir died on October 28, 1627. But in history, his name deserves special respect as a great emperor as well as an extraordinary ornithologist and astronomer.

It also goes to show that bird-watching and the scientific study of space and nature are so attractive that even an emperor forgets his kingship and becomes a humble and inquisitive researcher.

This also proves that there is such a wonderful charm in this world with diverse, colorful forms and beautiful images that it remains the same even after the passing of centuries. Great kings and emperors come and go, but people always remember this beautiful attraction of nature and those who love it.

❐

# 21

# Sawai Raja Jai Singh II

## Scholar of Indian astronomy
## (1686-1747)

The pinnacle and perfection at which Indian astronomy was in ancient times did not remain the same later. Many scholars consider the medieval period as the era of decline of Indian science and astronomy. However, there have also been several historically significant attempts to progress in this direction, beginning in the 18th century by understanding the achievements of Indian astronomy and integrating the knowledge of the East and the West. In this era, the name of Emperor Sawai Jai Singh II, who gave a new shape to the Indian astronomy of research and study in astronomy, cannot be forgotten. He discovered some wonderful instruments to know the position of sun and stars at the time and established Jantar-Mantar at various places and attracted the public to astronomy.

Born in 1686, Jaisingh was very studious and scholar despite being from the royal family. He befriended the Mughal emperor Aurangzeb. Aurangzeb was an admirer of his sharp intellect and bravery. After the death of Aurangzeb, Mohammad Shah ascended the throne. After some time Raja Jaisingh established a beautiful city — Jaipur. He got the guidance of his Guru Pandit

Jagannath in settling it. The establishment of Jaipur is very excellent and beautiful from the point of view of architecture. Meanwhile, Raja Jaisingh started studying the books of famous astronomers of the world by ordering them. The books of world famous astronomers like Tallimi, Ulugweg, John Flaxteed, and others were in his museum which he studied thoroughly.

After studying these texts, Raja Jai Singh also ordered telescopes. He himself also started making telescopes.

Raja Jaisingh had a wonderful yearning to observe the positions and motions of the moon and stars in space. Taking time out from all his activities, he used to study space. His study was so accurate that he found out and corrected the errors in the data of the earlier studies regarding the movements of the moon and stars. After this, for the study of the position and movements of the moon, sun and stars, he built Jantar-Mantar in Delhi and published his famous book 'Jin Mohammad Shahi' on astronomy. After this, he got Jantar-Mantar built in many other cities as well. Raja Jaisingh took its main idea from Ulugbeg. The design of the Jantar-Mantar built by him is very similar to Ulugbeg's observatory.

The original instruments that Raja Jaisingh discovered in his observatory and built according to his vision are Samrat-Yantra, Ram-Yantra and Jayaprakash. Among these yantras, the Samrat-Yantra is a sundial that tells the exact time. With this, the height of the Sun can also be measured. The height of the stars and their position is known from the Ram-Yantra. The position of all the planets can be measured by Jayaprakash. Jaisingh developed these instruments according to his original imagination. This allowed them to be considered far more correct and pure in their time. This is the reason why the observations and tables made by Jaisingh on the basis of these instruments seem more correct than those of world famous astronomers like Talini and Ulugbeg.

Raja Jaisingh also has some obvious limitations as an astronomer. Till now Earth was studied as the center of the universe and it was believed that all celestial bodies revolve around the Earth, but the great astronomer Copernicus proved with his revolutionary findings that the center of the universe is not the Earth, but the Sun, and all the planets revolve around the Sun. The assumption that the earth is stable is wrong. This revolutionary idea of Copernicus had come to the fore during the time of Raja Jaisingh. Nevertheless, Raja Jaisingh put forth his thoughts and concepts on the basis of the Earth-centric hypothesis of astronomy.

It is possible that he did this because of the fear of the priests, because in most of the religious texts also the earth is shown to be stable and the sun-moon revolving around it. Whatever may be the reality, despite being a talented astronomer, not being able to amend his belief would be considered as his weakness. Yet, surprisingly, many of his observations are accurate. The calculations of his Jantar-Mantar are scientifically correct and appropriate even today. This shows his flair and extraordinary talent as an astronomer.

This prodigious astronomer-emperor died on October 2, 1743. Of course, whenever India's most important astronomers are discussed, the name of Sawai Raja Jaisingh II will definitely be included in them. He really served as a useful link between ancient astronomy and modernity.

❐

# 22

# Pathani Samant

## Great astronomer of the 19th century (1835–1904)

Pathani Samanta, the great Indian astronomer of the 19th century, remained almost unknown despite his amazing personality and works. Very few people are familiar with his great achievements and work, while many of the world's well-known scientists have considered his presence as a wonder. This shows how apathetic and negligent the attitude of ourselves is towards the work, life-struggle and achievements of Indian scientists.

The full name of Pathani Samant was Mahamahopadhyay Pandit Samant Chandshekhar Harichandan Mohapatra. But most of the people used to call him as Pathani Samant. While living in the forests of Orissa completely different from the western lifestyle, by studying Indian astronomy and observing with his own eyes, he made such amazing conclusions and discovered astronomical principles that in today's time, one can't remain without being amazed at his work. It is more surprising when we learn that he did not even have a modest watch and there was no question of having telescope. Seeing everything with his own eyes, he came to know, drew conclusions from repeated observations and on the strength of immense hard work not only showed the theories and their shortcomings of ancient Indian scholars, but removed these shortcomings and created new theories. This revealed many mysteries of space and the motions of the planets.

Born on December 13, 1835 in Khandapada state of Odisha, Pathani Samant was a nature-lover since childhood and he loved to look at the images of nature and space; this created his interest in planets-satellites and space science. He did not even get the guidance of any qualified scholar in this regard. But yes, the texts of ancient scholars and astronomers guided him a lot.

Pathani's grandfather was the king of Khandapada. But despite being from the royal family, he did not get any help from the state and perhaps he never desired it. Proud of being a royal family, free from dominance, he remained engrossed in his tune. Study your way and live your way. He had immense power of talent. That's why the people whom he came in contact with, would definitely be surprised by his ability. In particular, Mahamahopadhyay Maheshchand Nyayaratna was greatly impressed by his astronomy and scholarship. After meeting Pathani Samant, he felt that a person with a blazing talent like lightning was standing in front of him. But he himself did not know much about astronomy, so he asked his friend Yogeshchand Rai to check the veracity of the words of Pathani Samant.

Yogeshchand Rai, after listening to the words of Pathani Samant, understood his arguments, principles and he was surprised to know the deep serious study behind them. The principles of Pathani Samant were so logical and correct that he felt it necessary to propagate it in the educated society, so that people could become familiar with the achievements, continuous research and its height of Indian astronomy. But the more Pathani Samant was immersed in studies, the more he had to stay away from publicity. Then only Yogeshchand Rai published his thoughts and his book with his editorial note and then the scientists of India and the world saw the brilliance of the Pathani Samant. Pathani Samant's conclusions were correct. His passion for astronomy is evident from the fact that wherever there was a possibility of a solar or lunar eclipse, he would walk miles and study the positions of the sun, moon and sky.

For this, he had also made some very original instruments for himself, by which he could compensate the absence of telescope to a great extent.

Pathani Samant gave form and shape to his entire study of astronomy in the book *'Siddhanta 'Darpan'*, which is a unique book of its kind. It contains commentaries on astronomical studies and theories of ancient scholars, corrections of their mistakes and then new revised theories are also given. Pathani Samant wrote this book in Sanskrit language on palm-leaf, but his script was Oriya script. Later his translations were published in English, so the attention of other scientists of the world also went towards him.

Knowledge-science journals of international importance like 'Nature' and 'Knowledge' have praised Pathani Samant's works, achievements and his unique astronomy. Later, the grandson of Pathani Samant wrote his biography, then it came to know about his life-struggle and difficulties, passing through which and suffering immense suffering, this great astronomer discovered his principles. Scientists in the countries like Germany, Britain, France, and America ordered this book written on Pathani Samant and a long process of research on his life and works started.

The small instruments made by Pathani Samant with the help of bamboo and sticks to see the night sky, shows his scientific understanding and originality. At least in the modern era, there has been no other astronomer with more original ideas than him. He died on June 11, 1904. It is a pity that we Indians know so little about such an extraordinary astronomer!

❒

# 23

# Sir Gangaram

## Great visionary engineer of India
## (1851–1927)

Sir Gangaram's name is taken with great respect among those brilliant, visionary engineers of India, who laid the foundation of a new and industrial India rich in scientific terms. He was a great patriot, but he believed that India could not progress without scientific progress. He said that if the stomach of the people of a country is hungry, then that country can never progress. And to feed the people, we have to develop the industries of the country. Sir Gangaram was such a clever and talented engineer that he was entrusted with big projects of country-building and he did such amazing things that even the British government was fascinated by his success. That is why he was honored with the title 'Sir'.

Born on April 13, 1851 in Mangatwali village of Sheikhpura district of Punjab, Gangaram was very intelligent, clever and studious since childhood. He was considered a prodigy child from the very beginning. His father Lala Daulatram was in the police. Later he came to Amritsar. Gangaram also studied first in

Amritsar and then in Lahore. He studied engineering at Thomson Engineering College, Roorkee. After this, he started working as an assistant engineer in Lahore.

After some time, when a plan was made to lay the Amritsar-Pathankot railway line, then Sir Gangaram was given the responsibility of completing it. He accomplished it very efficiently. After some time he became Executive Engineer in Lahore and completed many famous buildings including Heeramandi Waterworks, Gayo School of Arts and Cathedral. Even after retiring from this job, his steps did not stop. Impressed by his talent, he was called to Patiala. He built many buildings of historical importance including the Moti Bagh Palace and Secretariat there. Similarly, Malviya ji urged him to give advice for the construction of Banaras Hindu University. Its building structure was made according to his instructions.

But the more important work of Gangaram's life was yet to be done. It was such a charismatic act that later sowed the seeds of Green Revolution all over India. Sir Gangaram saw that a large part of the land of Punjab was lying barren due to lack of the means of irrigation. The reason was that the land was much higher than the surface of the rivers. How to irrigate it with river water? Gangaram said that today engineering has come to such a stage that 'Utkarsh Sinchai' i.e. irrigation of land several feet higher than the water surface is also possible. Everyone was surprised to hear this.

When Sir Gangaram talked about experimenting in this regard, he got a lot of land for this work. This land was in Layalpur and was eight to nine feet above the water-level of the city. He was engaged in his work even in the scorching heat of the day, burning day and night. It was also a difficult task to bring machines there. But Gangaram, as was his wont, did not waver. After all, he produced such a crop there and showed it that people thought, this is not reality, it is a dream! He was being praised everywhere in the country. Then, not only in Punjab, his unique method of irrigation was adopted in other parts of the country as well and the foundation of Green Revolution was laid in the whole country.

After this, Gangaram got the idea of generating electricity from water. He thought that many canals have been built in Punjab. Why can't electricity be made from them? The government gave him a huge barren land to complete his work and Gangaram started fulfilling his dreams.

He built a hydroelectric power house at Renlakhurd. Iron poles were placed at various places.

But the difficulty was that here the water used to fall from a height of only two feet, then how could it be made? At last a small canal was taken out of it. Then the arrangement was made so that the water started falling from six feet. After this, special type of turbines were installed. Steam powered machines were introduced. Miles long drains, canals and bridges were built and finally Sir Gangaram showed by generating electricity from falling water from such a low height. It was truly an amazing scientific charisma!

Sir Gangaram had a great yearning to serve the country. Whatever scientific ability he had, he used it in the innovation of the country. He had a dream that India should become industrially prosperous and he showed it by getting them done. He knew the pain of poverty, so serving the poor and helpless people seemed to him true patriotism. He created many institutions to help the poor and widows. He also did a lot of work to encourage the students in education.

For the purpose of treating the poor and providing proper medical facilities for the people of the country, Sir Gangaram got hospitals built at different places. Even today these hospitals are functioning well under the Sir Gangaram Trust. One of these hospitals is also in Delhi which is very well known and reputed.

Sir Gangaram, a great scientist with a big heart and big intentions, was engaged in his work like an ascetic till the last moment of his life. He breathed his last on 10th July 1927 at the age of 76. But the dream of a new, advanced India that this great visionary engineer had seen has been fulfilled to a large extent today.

❐

# 24

# Jagdishchandra Basu

## Leading scientist of modern India
## (1858–1937)

Jagdishchandra Basu is counted among the foremost scientists of modern India. Jagdishchandra Basu created a new history in the world of science by showing life in trees and plants and metals and other substances considered lifeless. On the one hand, he narrowed the wide gap between living and non-living, and on the other, eliminated the dividing line between science and philosophy and brought science closer to Indian thought and philosophy.

Jagdishchandra Basu was born on 30th November 1858 in a city named Mymensingh in Bengal (now Bangladesh). He had love for different types of animals since childhood. He liked to study their nature and lifestyle. Jagadishchandra Basu's father Bhagwanchandra Basu was the Deputy Collector. He did not like western civilization. So initially Jagadishchandra Basu was educated in such a school where he got an opportunity to live and play with tribals and poor rural children. Jagdishchandra Basu liked it and many of his rituals were formed here which kept guiding him throughout his life. He was later admitted to St. Xavier's School in Calcutta. There were many English and Anglo-Indian students here, who initially used to make fun of Jagadishchandra Basu and harass him.

One day, after being fed up, he had to beat up the evil boxer boy. But after this no one showed the courage to trouble him.

Jagdishchandra Basu's further studies took place at St. Xavier's College. It was here that he met Professor Father Lifant, who encouraged Jagadishchandra Basu to study physics and mathematics, but something else was going on inside Jagadishchandra Basu. He had immense love for animals. For this reason, he used to think of becoming a doctor. He took admission in Madison in London. But he got allergic to the chemicals used there. So he left his studies midway and returned.

He was then sent to study at Christ's College, Cambridge, where teachers such as Lord Raleigh, Francis Darwin, and Sydney Winia taught him. Within no time, new horizons of knowledge and science started opening within Jadgishchandra Basu. On coming to India, he was appointed to the post of Assistant Professor in Presidency College, Calcutta. Here Basu was getting half the salary compared to the Britishers. Research facilities were also not given. Basu did not even touch the salary for three years. Finally, the management committee of the college had to withdraw this wrong decision and Jagdishchandra Basu started getting salary equal to the English professors.

Basu now completely immersed himself in studies and research. He invented and successfully demonstrated the wireless telegraph. But the credit was given to Marconi for not patenting this discovery. Later, when a magazine in England published this, the attention of the whole world went towards Jagdishchandra Basu.

In 1900, the International Conference of Physics was held in Paris, in which Basu read his famous research paper. He insisted that it is wrong to call plants and metals inanimate. They also have the same life as seen in living beings. Yes, it needs to be looked at more carefully. He proved his mettle by using it on carrot and turnip leaves. Later he went to London at the invitation of the Linnean Society and read his research paper. His paper was initially rejected by the Royal Society. But later it was accepted for publication.

After this, Basu's fame reached more heights. In no time, his idea spread all over the world that the gulf between living and non-living things is not as wide as is unfortunately understood.

Basu used to say that when plants can breathe without lungs, digest food without stomach and muscles, then why can't they feel without nervous system? They also have the same sensitivity as humans. To study the effect of stimuli and sensitivity of plants, Basu made many amazing instruments like Resonant Recorder, Phytograph Photosynthetic Recorder and Crescograph. The specialty of these instruments was that they could show the growth of plants or the effects on them by multiplying them. In the beginning there were many who ridiculed Basu's idea. But gradually all the serious scientists accepted his opinion. Jagdishchandra Basu became famous all over the world.

Jagdishchandra Basu died on 23 November 1937. But the work of this great scientist, who hoisted the flag of science in modern India, will continue to guide us for centuries to come.

❒

# 25

# Prafulla Chandra Ray

## Great Chemist of Modern India
## (1861–1944)

Prafulla Chandra Ray is one of those sages of modern India, who, despite suffering a lot, paved the way for India's scientific progress with his deep understanding and connected it deeply with the welfare and service of the people. Therefore, science was also a means of serving humanity for him. The personality of this great scientist who laid the foundation of chemistry in modern India was so simple that people were amazed to see it. Taking inspiration from him, thousands of young men were attracted towards science and many of them became eminent scientists.

Born on August 2, 1861 in Raduli village of Khulna district, Prafulla Chandra Ray was very intelligent and dedicated since childhood and was immersed in his studies most of the time. His father Harishchandra Ray was a distinguished person and a scholar of Persian. He was of the opinion that we should learn both English and Indian languages. Balanced development of personality can be achieved only by getting both western and Indian knowledge. Due to his interest in the promotion of education, he had opened a school in his village itself. Initially Prafulla Chandra Ray studied in this school. Later, when his father came to Kolkata, Prafulla Chandra Ray got education in Hare School of Kolkata. After some time, his studies stopped due to being seriously unwell, but while staying at home, Prafulla Chandra Ray read the works of Gold Smith, Edison, etc.

This hobby of reading and writing remained in him till the end and it brought openness in his personality. In those days he also got attracted towards Brahmo Samaj. He used to listen to Keshav Chand Sen's enthusiastic lectures with great interest.

After studying at Presidency College, Calcutta, he went to England for further studies and studied for six years in Edinburgh. From there he achieved D.Sc., the highest degree of science. After returning to India, he kept in his mind that whatever it may be, India should be taken forward on the path of progress of science. He was of the firm opinion that only through science can India move forward and get its count among the leading nations of the world. He believed that India was very advanced scientifically in ancient times. But later, in the name of religion in India, stereotypes and bigotry emerged, which put a big obstacle in the way of scientific development of the country. This is how this country went towards downfall.

People were amazed to read these thoughts of Prafulla Chandra Ray and the attention of the whole world went towards the works and inventions of the ancient scientists of India. Based on these thoughts and doing a lot of research, he wrote his great book *'History of Hindu Chemistry'*, which created a lot of stir and attracted the attention of thousands of scientists from India and abroad. By reading this, it is known that in ancient times India was ahead of the whole world in science. Such discoveries had been made here in chemistry and alchemy, which were not known to other countries till much later.

Prafulla Chandra Ray himself made many such important scientific discoveries, which influenced the scientists of the whole world. Especially in 1895, with the discovery of mercuric nitrate, Prafulla Chandra Ray's name spread rapidly in the world of science. In this way, thanks to the efforts of Dr. Ray, in the field of scientific achievements, the name of India was also taken with respect in the world.

Prafulla Chandra Ray did not just say, but he used to do what he said. This is the reason that not only did he do remarkable work in the field of science, he also continued to help science students.

As a professor of science, he would get a good salary, but he would take a little of it for his living. The rest of the money he used to give as scholarships to science students. Even if there was a problem in paying the fees or any other difficulty, even when he himself was in trouble, he used to give money on his behalf and encourage the students to study further and work.

To take India forward in the field of chemistry, Dr. Ray established the Bengal Chemical Works with a very small capital, which made a lot of progress in no time. Prafulla Chandra Ray's understanding and penance was now accepted by everyone.

Many people were his devotees. Among his disciples were Meghnad Saha, Rasiklal Dutt and Neelratan Dhar, who went on to do a lot of work and earn fame. Prafulla Chandra Ray had such a deep influence on the youth of Bengal that sometimes people asked him to join politics. To this he used to reply, "The country also needs scientists. When thirty chemists are born in the country, then I will leave my work and start working in politics."

It is no less surprising that on the one hand, Prafulla Chandra Ray was a strong advocate of the scientific development of the country, and on the other, he strongly supported Gandhiji's spinning wheel. He believed that even if the spinning wheel could not stand in front of the big mills, it could be of great service to the poor people.

This great chemist of India passed away on June 16, 1944. He was a true son of the country, who lived every moment for the scientific progress of the country. The truth is that the way India has progressed scientifically today, it would never have been possible if it had not been for the guidance of sages like Dr. Prafulla Chandra Ray.

Truly, he was such a scientist, who can be called the 'Sage of Modern Science'.

❒

# 26

# Mokshagundam Visvesvaraya

## A great imaginative engineer
## (1861-1962)

Mokshagundam Visvesvaraya is counted among the great engineers of India, who not only had deep knowledge of science, but also had a strong feeling of patriotism in his heart and yearning to live and die for the development of the country. The truth is that Mokshagundam Visvesvaraya contributed no less to the progress of the country by building giant dams on rivers and opening steel factories than the great freedom fighters and politicians of India who served the country by participating in the freedom struggle.

Born on September 15, 1861 in Madanahalli village of Kolar district of Karnataka, Visvesvaraya was very studious since childhood. His parents were poor, who could not afford his education. That's why they were arranging their fees, etc. by teaching tuition. The English principal of his college was mesmerised by his talent. He wrote a letter in praise of him. This not only got him admission in engineering college, but also started getting a stipend. This made the way easier for Visvesvaraya and day and night, he immersed himself in his studies.

After completing his engineering studies, Visvesvaraya started working as an assistant engineer in the Public Works Department of Mumbai. Before his candidness, the higher officials were somewhat annoyed, but as soon as they came to know about Visvesvaraya's ability and qualities to work, they started praising him fiercely. After this, he kept getting higher positions one by one. Visvesvaraya took up the tasks which even the British officers were afraid to do and got them done quickly.

After being relieved from government service, Visvesvaraya started working as a special consultant engineer in the princely state on the request of the Hyderabad government. At that time, the Nizam of Hyderabad was troubled by the flood situation there, due to which the public was suffering a lot and the princely state was suffering huge loss of life and property. Sensing the problem, Visvesvaraya got the Krishnaraja dam built on the Kaveri river. It was such a huge and magnificent dam that seeing this miracle of Visvesvaraya, everyone woke up with applause. With the construction of this dam, the public got a lot of water and electricity facility.

After some time, working on the post of Dewan of Mysore State, Visvesvaraya established more than one chain of factories in the state. Visvesvaraya's fame had spread so far that at the age of 92 he was asked to advise on a bridge being built over the Ganges at Mokama in Bihar.

Visvesvaraya had grown up quite a lot, but even at this stage he did enough study by visiting the construction site himself and visiting the surrounding area there. And finally, he succeeded in completing a big task. In 1955, he was awarded the 'Bharat Ratna', the highest title given by the Government of India.

Visvesvaraya had a long life. On 14th April 1962, at the age of 101, this great scientist and talented engineer of India, who lived a simple life like a saint, passed away.

Visvesvaraya's name and work are still discussed with great respect among the great personalities who laid the foundation stone for a new India.

❐

# 27

# Dr. Ganesh Prasad

## Prominent Mathematician of Modern India (1876–1935)

Dr. Ganesh Prasad's name is prominent among the great mathematicians of modern India who attracted the attention of the whole world with his intelligence and talent and whose name is taken with respect. He was such an exceptionally talented scientist, whose rise the world saw as a surprise and whose many research articles and installations are still used in new research in mathematics. Not only this, Ganesh Prasad was such a brilliant person who devoted every moment of his life to create an environment suitable for modern mathematics and science all over India.

Born on November 15, 1876 in Ballia Nagar, Uttar Pradesh, Dr. Ganesh Prasad was different from others since childhood. Due to his extraordinary talent, everyone's attention used to go towards him. Despite this, he failed in mathematics in the fifth grade. This shocked the boy Ganesh Prasad so much that he started working day and night to read and understand mathematics. Soon he acquired such mastery in mathematics that he used to help the students of classes older than him in their difficulties in mathematics. He got married during his student days.

After the sudden demise of his wife, he refused to remarry and lovingly raised his little daughter. Only a few days were left for his M.A. examination when suddenly the daughter also passed away. Ganesh Prasad was heartbroken. But somehow he overcame his grief and went for the exam and when the result came, people were amazed. He passed in first class. From Allahabad University, he had done B.Sc. degree. Then went to Cambridge University for further research under a scholarship. There Klopman, a great scholar of mathematics, was very impressed by the talent of Dr. Ganesh Prasad. He used to say, "In the form of Ganesh Prasad, such a star has risen in the world of mathematics, who will dim the light of all the stars before him!"

Dr. Ganesh Prasad was still a student when his research papers started getting published in important magazines and journals of the country and abroad and the attention of many well-known scientists was attracted towards him. One of his research papers *'Elliptical Functions and Spherical Harmonics'* is very famous. In this research paper, he has shown the mistakes of great mathematicians and while improving their conclusions, he has given his new and original installations. After the publication of this research paper, the attention of mathematicians and scientists of the whole world went towards him and he got praise from all sides. He received an invitation from Germany to come there. On reaching Germany, world famous mathematician George Kantor himself came to meet Ganesh Prasad. He blessed Ganesh Prasad and said, "May the fragrance of your fame spread like the fragrance of musk."

After obtaining a degree from Cambridge, Dr. Ganesh Prasad went to the town of Naatgarn in Germany, where he did research work at a high level with the scholars of mathematics like Jamal Field and Hilbard. After returning to India from there, he started teaching mathematics at Mayur Center College, Allahabad. After some time he was appointed at Queens College, Kashi. Ashutosh Mukherjee, the Vice-Chancellor of the University of Calcutta, recognized his talent and appointed him as Professor of Applied Mathematics at the University of Calcutta.

Even while living here, Dr. Ganesh Prasad's studies and his discoveries regarding mathematics continued continuously. His work regarding the Fourier series is still considered amazing.

Among his books, *'A Treatise on Differential Equations'* and *'On the Constitution of Matter and Analytical Theories of Heat'* are famous. These have been considered books for researching new horizons in mathematics. Even today, they are read with great interest in the country and abroad.

Another very important work which immortalized the fame of Dr. Ganesh Prasad is the establishment of Agra University. Not only did he play a central role in the establishment of Agra University, but as a member of its Senate, he worked hard to make it more level-headed and disciplined.

He died on March 9, 1935 while participating in the meeting of the Senate. There he had to speak a lot to make his point effectively. When he sat down after saying his words, he could not get up again. He was immediately taken to the hospital, where he passed away at 7.30 in the evening. Mathematicians and researchers from India and abroad always remember this extraordinary scholar and master of mathematics respectfully.

❐

# 28

# Dr. Darashaw Noshervan Wadia

Remarkable geologist
(1883–1969)

Among the scientists of modern India, the number of scholars who specialize by working with a keen interest in geology is not very large. But stalwarts like Dr. Darashaw Noshervan Wadia have proved that Indian talents can hoist their fame in any field if they want. All the surveys done in India from the point of view of geology were done by foreigners only. But when Dr. Darashaw Noshervan Wadia took interest and mastered this field, then for the first time the reports and findings of the Indian land survey came out from the Indian point of view, which really played a big role in the development of India. In this context, the work of Dr. Wadia is so important that geologists from all over the world have appreciated him.

Born on October 23, 1887 in Surat city of Gujarat, Darashaw Noshervan Wadia was very clever and talented since childhood. After passing the examinations of B.Sc. and M.A. from University of Mumbai, he became interested in geology, so he started reading books in this regard. His aim was to do such a geological study of India, which would play a big role in its development. Dr. Wadia wished that the young generation should also come forward to work enthusiastically in this direction. Therefore, when he was appointed as Professor of Geology in Prince of Wales, Jammu, he greatly encouraged the young generation towards this unknown subject.

In this context, he also wrote an informative and interesting book like *'Geology for Students'*, which is still considered a very useful and important book in this direction.

After some time, he was appointed in the Indian Geological Survey Department (Geological Survey of India). There, he did many challenging tasks. He became the National Professor of Geology and a member of the Planning Commission. Dr. Wadia's original genius attracted the attention of scholars and researchers everywhere. His ideas about the Pir Panjal ranges of Punjab were considered important by many geologists of the world.

Similarly, after an in-depth study of the structure of the vast ranges of the Himalayas, he gave his important findings. The mountain ranges of the Himalayas turn towards Burma with such a sharp turn that it seems that they cannot be one mountain range, but two mountain ranges have merged together. But Dr. Wadia, after an in-depth study of the rocks of both the mountain ranges, proved that these are the mountain ranges of the Himalayas and the thesis of meeting of the two mountain ranges is not correct. Similarly, one by one difficult and challenging scientific research was done by Dr. Wadia, due to which India's achievements from geological point of view could emerge in front of the whole world.

Dr. Wadia was a serious scholar and he gave many such principles from geological point of view, which solved many old knots and riddles of geology. Dr. Wadia believed that there was an ice age ten million years ago and its remains are found in the form of sand at the North Pole. Among the important books written by Dr. Wadia are *'Geology of India and Burma'*, *'Geology of Naga Parvat and Gilgit District Structure of Himalaya'*. Geologists around the world consider them extremely useful and important.

Dr. Darashaw Noshervan Wadia was exceptionally talented as well as a very hard worker. He remained engaged in his work till the end and inspired and encouraged others to do new research in this field.

This great geologist of India passed away on June 15, 1969. But by making new surprising discoveries in geology, India's fame-flag waved all over the world from geological point of view; it will always challenge the new generation to move forward and do something new.

❐

# 29

# Srinivasa Ramanujan

## World-renowned mathematician of India
## (1887-1920)

Srinivasa Ramanujan's name is first taken among the great mathematicians of India's modern age. The work done by this exceptionally brilliant mathematician in a short life of just 33 years can never be forgotten. If someone calls Srinivasa Ramanujan the 'Bhaskaracharya of the modern age', then nothing will be wrong.

Srinivasa Ramanujan was born on December 22, 1887 in Erode, a small village in Madras province. The economic condition of the house was not particularly good. Initially he studied in a rural school. Then he was sent to study at Kumbakonam High School. There the teachers noticed that this child named Srinivasa Ramanujan often remained silent and kept thinking something in his mind. Not only this, sometimes his questions were such that even the teachers used to get confused. Somehow they had to get rid of the boy. Once upon a time, a teacher was telling the class that if a number is divided by the same number, the answer is always one. Then suddenly

Ramanujan got up and asked, "Will zero divided by zero still give the answer one?" The teacher immediately realised his mistake and agreed that it would rather come to an indefinite number or infinity.

Similarly, Ramanujan would often ask questions about the circumference of the earth or the distance between the constellations, etc. His classmates or teachers thought him crazy. While the truth was that the 'great mathematician of the future' sitting inside Ramanujan used to show a small glimpse of himself through these questions.

Situation was that despite the lack of resources, this passion of Ramanujan kept increasing continuously. In the fourth grade, he had not only started studying trigonometry, but had also achieved great mastery in it. He asked a student of B.A. to lend him his trigonometry book for a few days. He agreed with great difficulty to give this book to them. But one day he was surprised to see that Ramanujan was solving trigonometry problems indiscriminately. Then the situation happened that if a B.A. class student faced any difficulty, he had to take help from Ramanujan.

In high school, Ramanujan got such good marks in mathematics that he started getting government scholarship. But gradually he was getting so engrossed in mathematics that he started lagging behind in other subjects. The situation was such that the stipend and Ramanujan's studies stopped midway.

After some time Ramanujan got married, but he was troubled due to financial difficulties. He met V. Ramaswami Iyer, the founder of the Indian Mathematical Society, and asked him to get him a small job. Ramaswami Iyer sent him to P.V. Seshuiyer. He got a tutoring job to make ends meet. Then Seshuiyer sent him to Dewan Bahadur Acharya Ramchandra Rao. When Ramanujan met Rao Saheb, at first he avoided seeing his dirty clothes and strange condition. But in the very next meeting, when Ramanujan showed him the most difficult problems he had solved, he was shocked. He understood that Ramanujan was an exceptionally brilliant young man who had made such important discoveries in mathematics whom no one in the world knows about yet. Ramachandra Rao told Ramanujan, "I will take care of you until you get a decent job." But Ramanujan did not accept this. Then with the efforts of Ramachandra Rao, Ramanujan got a job as a clerk at a salary of thirty rupees a month.

Meanwhile Ramachandra Rao wrote a letter to Sir Francis Spring telling him about this brilliant mathematician. Sir Francis Spring showed Dr. G.V. Walker, Director of Government Observatories, Ramanujan's mathematical work and the new principles he had discovered. Walker was absolutely amazed. He wrote to the registrar of the University of Madras asking him to grant a scholarship to this exceptionally brilliant mathematician. The result of this letter was that Ramanujan started getting a scholarship of seventy-five rupees a month. Meanwhile, many of his articles were published in the letter of the Indian Mathematical Society and they became famous.

Now Ramanujan was so engrossed in his practice of mathematics that he didn't even aware of his food and drink. On the request of some friends, he wrote his articles to world famous mathematician Dr. G.H. Hardy. Hardy mentioned a number in one of his articles. He wrote that so far the expression for a prime number smaller than this number could not be discovered. But Ramanujan had already found him. When Ramanujan sent him his article about this, Hardy was amazed. The most surprising thing was that Ramanujan's method of solving the problem was very original and his own and till now no one had any idea about it.

Dr. Hardy had a great desire that Ramanujan should somehow come to England, so that he could do his work more quickly and the whole world could know about his amazing discovcries. But Ramanujan was still hesitating. One reason for this was the behaviour of his family members and relatives. They threatened to boycott him if he went abroad.

Still, Hardy was constantly trying to call him to England. When the scientist of mathematics E.H. Neville came to India, Hardy also asked him to meet Ramanujan and persuade him to come to England. Still, Hardy was constantly trying to call him to England. Neville met Ramanujan and explained to him that on reaching England he would do further work for him. There will be many opportunities. Ramanujan's answer to this was, "I will ask mother. If she will give permission then only I will be able to go to England."

Ramanujan's mother was not ready at first, but then one night she had a dream that her son was sitting in a huge building and scholars from all over the world, including the British, were paying special respect to him. The mother understood that her son was destined to some special work. She allowed her son to go to England.

The company of Dr. Hardy in England gave great strength to Ramanujan. They got involved in their work with quadruple power. Even in England, Ramanujan's living was very simple. He used to eat simple food prepared by himself and was engrossed in his work day and night. His articles were now being published with great respect in the best journals of mathematics in the world and his name was added to the world's greatest mathematicians.

However, his health was deteriorating due to such hard work. Even then he did not worry about his health at all and was doing tireless mental labor. Due to this, he suffered from tuberculosis and after some time he became very weak. Ramanujan had understood that now he would not survive. Even then, on his deathbed, he was busy trying to solve the unsolved problems of mathematics.

Once Dr. Hardy came to visit him in the hospital. His room number in the hospital was 1729. Dr. Hardy said humorously, "Oh, in what a wretched room number you're living!"

Ramanujan laughed at this and said, "That's a very interesting number. Look at it as the sum of two cubes of different types. The sum of the cubes of 10 and 9 and 12 and 1 is 1729."

Hardy was overjoyed to hear that. He was surprised that even in this condition, Ramanujan's intelligence and mathematical talent were so active.

This great mathematician passed away on April 26, 1920 in a village in Madras. After his death, a collection of his articles was published from Cambridge University Press, which is still read and inspired by the connoisseurs of mathematics with great respect and devotion.

❐

# 30

# Chandrasekhara Venkataraman

## Top Scientist of Modern India (1888–1970)

Among the top scientists of modern India, the name of Chandrasekhara Venkataraman first comes to mind. Apart from being a great and incredible scientist, he was humble and simple, one for whom the living-ideal is deeply entrenched in Indianness. When in 1930, Raman was awarded the Nobel Prize, the biggest honor of the world, he became not only the first Indian scientist to receive this award, but also the first Asian scientist.

Chandrasekhara Venkataraman was born on 7 November 1888 in Ayyanpettai village in Tiruchirappalli district of Tamil Nadu. His father Chandrasekhar Iyer was a teacher. Mother's name was Parvati Ammal. Since childhood, Raman was intelligent in studies and used to ask such questions in the class that often his teachers used to get confused. When Raman was studying in B.A. in Presidency College, E. H. Elliot, who came to teach English, was surprised to see him. Seeing this thin student of small height, he felt that perhaps a child of a small class had come and sat in the class by mistake. But when he spoke to Raman, he was greatly pleased by his polite and intelligent answers.

Raman was very sensible in his student life. At the age of only sixteen, he discovered the diffraction band by measuring the angle of the prism with a spectrometer. After writing an article on this, he showed it to Professor Johnson. When he did not reply, Raman sent it to the Philosophical Magazine published from London. As soon as that article was published in the magazine, Raman's fame spread everywhere. After this, his another article related to surface tension was published in this magazine. Only then did his correspondence with the famous scientist Lord Raleigh begin. Initially, Lord Raleigh thought him to be a professor of Presidency College. But later on, when the truth came to know, he praised the talent of this prodigy child.

After studies, Raman was appointed to the post of Deputy Accountant General in Calcutta. Then he gradually became the Accountant General of the Telegraph Department. But Raman was not satisfied. His mind was running towards the study and research of science. He was associated with the 'Indian Association for the Cultivation of Science'. But he was not able to give as much time as he wanted to the organization. In those days, he received an offer from Calcutta University to accept the post of Sir Taraknath Palit Professor. This salary was half of what Raman was getting at that time. Nevertheless, Raman happily accepted the position and quickly got involved in his work.

In 1921, Raman was sent as a representative of Calcutta University in the University Conference to be held in Chicago.

There Raman got a chance to meet many great scientists of the world including Rutherford. While returning, Raman's attention went towards the blue color of the Mediterranean Sea. Since childhood, he used to think, why is the color of the sky and the sea water so blue? The same question kept bothering him again and again. He had read Lord Raleigh's explanation about this. Lord Raleigh had called the blue of the sea a 'shade of the blue of the sky' but Raman was not satisfied with it. He immediately took out the prism and peeped through it, ' Hey, the colour of the sea is still visible as blue! That means it is not the effect of the sky. This blueness is coming from inside the water itself.'

After returning from there, Raman began to think more deeply about this matter. At the same time, his research was going on continuously. Suddenly, his attention was drawn to the fact that the Crompton effect which is true for X-ray rays, should also be true for light rays. That is, just as the nature of X-ray rays changes after passing through different mediums, the same can happen with light rays as well.

Raman's experiments soon proved that the form of rays of light changes when passing through different mediums. Raman's experiment was successful despite very modest equipment. He sent his article in this regard to the journal *'Nature'*, which published it under the name *'A New Type of Secondary Radiation'*. Soon this discovery of Raman spread all over the world. For this he received the highest honor Nobel Prize in 1930 and this effect on light rays was known as 'Raman effect'.

Apart from this, another important discovery of Raman was research on musical instruments like Veena, Violin, Mridangam. He gave a beautiful explanation of how such beautiful and harmonious music emerges from instruments like Mridangam.

Raman was proud to be an Indian, but it was very sad to see that Indians have very little share in the latest discoveries of modern science. In this India, he did the important work of motivating and guiding the young generation of scientists. Raman's dream was that there should be such an institution in the country, where students could research on the mysteries of space and universe etc. His wish was finally fulfilled in 1951. Raman Research Institute was established in Bangalore. In 1954, this top scientist of India was awarded the title of 'Bharat Ratna'.

On November 21, 1970, at the age of 82, this great scientist passed away. But he was active till the end and left behind a dream that will always inspire many scientists to understand the mysteries of life and the world.

❒

# 31

# Birbal Sahni

## The Great paleobotanist of India
## (1891-1949)

Birbal Sahni's name cannot be forgotten among the famous scientists of modern India. As a researcher of ancient flora, the name of Dr. Birbal Sahni is taken with great respect not only in India but all over the world.

Birbal Sahni was born on November 14, 1891 in Bhera village of Shahpur district of Punjab (now in Pakistan). His father Lala Ruchiram Sahni was a chemistry professor at the Government College. He was of progressive views and was counted among the prominent leaders of Brahmo Samaj. Birbal Sahni was also influenced by his father's personality. Since childhood, he used to be at the forefront of studies. He went to England in 1911 after completing his bachelor's degree in Botany from the Central College, Lahore. There he got a chance to work on Natural Sciences. He started his research work on fossil plants. It was here that he met Professor Albert C. Seward, who himself was involved in research on fossil plants. A deep intimate relationship developed between the two. Prof. Seward guided Birbal Sahni in every way. Birbal Sahni's research papers were published in famous research journals and soon his name came to be known as the chief researcher of ancient plants. In 1919, London University, recognizing the special importance of Birbal Sahni's work, awarded him D.Sc. degree.

After returning to India, Birbal Sahni worked for some time at Banaras Hindu University and then at Punjab University. In 1921, he was appointed to the post of Professor in the Botany Department of Lucknow University. He got a chance to work here for a long time.

One specialty of Birbal Sahni was that he loved simplicity and was engrossed in his work all the time. He did not like false ostentation or show of work. Once upon a time, a foreigner came to meet him; he had heard the name of Birbal Sahni a lot. On coming to Lucknow University he asked someone about Virbal Sahni's room, the person pointed towards the verandah. While he was busy in his work in a corner with his eyes fixed on the microscope, the foreigner asked in surprise, "Dr. Sahni, don't you have a room of your own?" Birbal Sahni's answer to this was, "What is the need of it? Great inventions can be done even sitting on a small attic." The foreigner was surprised to hear.

There are many stories of Dr. Sahni's sense of humour. Once he was working on *Azolla pinnata*, a microscopic aquatic plant. Suddenly his friend Dr. Sen asked him during the conversation, "Do you have azolla?" Sahni said with a smile, "Yes, why not." He immediately went inside and brought a sample of Azolla fossils. Moving towards Sen, he said very innocently, "Look, just hold him carefully, the poor man is only six crore years old now!"

Birbal Sahni was fond of traveling long distances. Many times in such journeys, he used to get rare species of plants, old things and fossils. He used to keep the students with him and filling them with enthusiasm, he used to tell them about those fossils.

Birbal Sahni donated his entire property to a society of archaeologists. The foundation of this Palaeobotanical Institute was laid by Pt. Jawaharlal Nehru. It was a dream come true for Birbal Sahni but alas, he passed away a week later on April 10, 1949. Then his wife Mrs. Savitri Sahni took over the responsibility.

Even today, this institute reminds us of this great palaeobotanist and encourages to do something new.

❐

# 32

# Dr. Meghnad Saha

## The Visionary Scientist
## (1893-1956)

In the modern era, Dr. Meghnad Saha is counted among the leading scientists who worked hard to make India a scientifically prominent and progressive country and made tireless efforts to popularize science among the youth of the country. Meghnad Saha was a famous scientist as well as a patriot, whose heart was restless every moment for the progress and prosperity of his country. Even for him, science was only a means of new construction of the country and service to humanity.

Born on October 6, 1893 in Seoratli village of Dhaka district, Dr. Meghnad Saha was fond of reading books and doing something new since childhood. The circumstances of the house were not good, but Meghnad Saha had high dreams and wanted to do something. At the same time, the spirit of patriotism was deeply filled within him. He used to get sad seeing the condition of the people of his country. When the British partitioned Bengal, a wave of anger ran across the country. Meghnad Saha was a student then, but he too was feeling a deep yearning within himself. He soon found a way to express his anger. It so happened that the British Governor of Bengal was about to come to his school, all the children were told that they must come to school that day. But Meghnad Saha deliberately did not go to school that day.

Consequently, his name was struck off from the school. Not only this, the stipend he was getting for studies was stopped and this made Meghnad Saha's financial conditions even more difficult. But he was not bothered by it even an iota. He was happy that he had expressed the anger of the whole country against the British even in symbolic form.

Meghnad Saha was a brilliant student. That's why in the second school where he got admission, he came first there too. This increased his confidence further. Later, he went to Presidency College, Kolkata for further studies, where he got the support and blessings of India's top scientists like Jagadishchandra Basu and Prafulla Chandra Ray. There were brilliant students like Satyendranath Bose, P.C. Mahalanobis who went on to do great things and earned fame all over the world.

After college studies, the question arose in front of Saha that what should he do next? The financial condition of the family was really bad and all eyes were on Meghnad Saha. But due to his close association with freedom fighters like Subhash Chandra Bose and Dr. Rajendra Prasad, he did not get a government job. Then he got involved in research work. Meanwhile, by teaching tuition, he started working somehow. In 1917, he became a professor at the University College of Science. But his aim was not to get a job by following a tightrope walk. Therefore, he took interest in the latest discoveries happening in physics. Relativity, thermodynamics and nuclear theory were his favorite subjects, on which he liked to collect the latest information and read new books. He studied the color sequence (spectrum) formed when sunlight emerges from a prism, etc. He also explained the spectral lines of lesser and greater thickness formed from it. With the formula given by him in this regard, the pressure, temperature etc. of Sun and other stars can be detected through spectral lines. This invention of Meghnad Saha created a stir among scientists working on light-space and star-physics. He had really found a solution to a big problem. However, when Meghnad Saha made this invention, he was only a young man of twenty-five-year old. His discovery got a place in some of the major and historical discoveries made in the field of Astrophysics.

Within no time, Meghnad Saha started being counted among the well-known scientists of astrophysics. In 1927, he was elected a member of the Royal Society. After getting appointment in Allahabad University, he immersed himself in study-teaching and his research work day and night. But at the same time, he used to continuously encourage young scientists to do new things. On coming to Kolkata from there, he did his research work on radio waves coming from the Sun and radio activation, which was considered an important work in this direction.

He had great interest in atomic theory and realized its increasing importance over time. He believed that atomic energy could be used for the new construction of the country and for large-scale creative works. Continuous research and hard work is needed. In this sense, he laid the foundation of the 'Institute of Nuclear Physics' which has done really important work in this direction.

Meghnad Saha was not simply a scientist. The pain and suffering of the poor people of the country was constantly churning for him and he wanted to see India progressing continuously. For this, he did not even hesitate to go into politics. In 1952, he contested and won the elections for the Parliament.

People loved him very much. Because even after being such a great scientist, there was no proud in him. He was down to earth personality. People could freely share their sorrows and problems to him. Dr. Saha used to address them if these were under his control. Surprisingly, despite all this, he used to work day and night doing his scientific research.

This visionary and dynamic scientist passed away on February 16, 1956 at the age of 63. But the hopeful dream he had of making India an advanced scientific country has been accomplished to a greater extent. The scientists of the present generation of a grateful nation still remember him with respect.

❐

# 33

# Satyendranath Bose

## The scientist who is called Einstein of India (1894–1974)

Satyendranath Bose is also one of the exceptionally brilliant scientists of modern India. The rare discovery he made together with the great scientist Einstein is called Bose-Einstein statistics. Not only this, Einstein himself got his scientific articles translated into German and got them printed with respect. This was a major achievement in the life of Satyendranath Bose and due to this, his fame spread all over the world as a scientist of extraordinary merit.

Satyendranath Bose, born in Kolkata on January 1, 1894, was very intelligent and bright since childhood. He was so smart, especially in mathematics, that it is said that Upendranath Bakshi, the mathematics teacher in the school, gave him one hundred and ten out of a hundred in the mathematics question paper. Later, while studying at Presidency College, Kolkata, Satyendranath Bose came in contact with brilliant scientists like Jagdishchandra Bose and Prafulla Chandra Ray. Since then a desire arose in his mind to do some great work in the field of science.

When the new Science College of Calcutta University opened, Satyendranath Bose was appointed as a lecturer there.

But Satyendranath was not happy with the old pattern of studies. He understood the new discoveries that were being made in physics, and used to tell about them to the students with great interest. When he met German scientist P.J. Bruhan, he started getting new books of science to read. In 1920, he translated Einstein's paper on the Theory of Relativity from German to English.

While Satyendranath Bose was in Berlin, one of his friends asked him to apply for the post of Reader at the University of Dacca, but Satyendranath Bose was reluctant, as he did not have a doctoral degree. His friend suggested, "If Einstein issued you a letter recommending your name, then the work will be done." Satyendranath Bose hesitantly said this to Einstein. Einstein was very surprised. He said, "You have done so much work. Do you still need the certificate?" Einstein immediately wrote the letter and Satyendranath Bose was appointed to the post of Reader in Dhaka University.

Even after this, the research work of Satyendranath Bose continued. In 1924, he wrote his important research article, *'Planck's Law and Light Quantum Hypothesis'* regarding the famous scientist Max Planck's 'Theory of Quantum'. This article was sent for publication in many reputed journals. But when it was returned from everywhere, Satyendranath Bose sent it to Einstein. Einstein liked the article so much that he himself translated it into German and published it with great respect. After this, Bose's name suddenly became famous all over the world. This research paper of Bose had a major role in the discovery of quantum statistics. This statistic was named Bose-

Einstein statistics. Also, the fundamental particles following Bose statistics were named 'bosons' on the lines of photons.

Apart from Einstein, Satyendranath Bose also got a chance to work with Madame Curie. When he met Madame Curie and told her his wish, she said hesitantly, "Learn French first." To this Bose replied in French, "Madam, I know French." Hearing this, Madame Curie happily included him in her working colleagues.

Satyendranath Bose was one of those scientists for whom science was not a separate thing. His whole life was full of science; the yearning to know and understand new scientific discoveries and works that were being done, and to connect new scientific discoveries with life remained in his mind till the end. He inspired many people to come forward and work for scientific studies and discoveries. Anyone who met him could not remain unimpressed by his passionate thoughts and profound scholarship.

In 1974, at a grand ceremony in Calcutta to honor Satyendranath Bose at the age of 80, he said, "My discoveries have been accepted by the world today. The purpose of my life is fulfilled. What will I do by living anymore?" "

He passed away exactly a month later on February 4, 1974. But we still feel and are thrilled by the extraordinary talent and brilliance of Satyendranath Bose.

❐

# 34

# Shanti Swarup Bhatnagar

## Pioneer of India's Scientific Progress (1894–1955)

Shanti Swarup Bhatnagar's name is also taken with great respect among the successful and famous scientists of modern India. Dr. Bhatnagar's work and role is very important in taking India forward on the path of progress of science. He can be called the great charioteer or *sarthavahak* of science in independent India, due to which India progressed so rapidly in industrial development. Shanti Swarup Bhatnagar was the first scientist in India to dream and plan for it.

Shanti Swaroop Bhatnagar was born on 21st February, 1894, in Bhera village of Shahpur district (now in Pakistan). He belonged to a very prestigious family. But his father was a follower of Brahmo Samaj. Due to his independent thoughts and self-respect, he rejected many high posts and accepted the post of headmaster in a high school. For this reason, the elders of the house evicted him from the ancestral property. Shanti Swarup Bhatnagar's childhood was spent in deprivation and poverty. After the death of the father, the condition became even more pathetic, the mother took him to her maternal home, Secunderabad (District Bulandshahr). It was here that studies of Shanti Swarup started.

He reached Lahore for further studies. There his talent in both science and Urdu came to the fore in such a way that even his teachers did not get tired of praising him. In his student life, he used to take great pleasure in doing interesting experiments of science; he had written about one such experiment in the letter 'Leader', which attracted the attention of many scientists and scholars. Everyone praised him.

Dr. Bhatnagar had a dream that India should progress on the path of industrial development through new discoveries of science. In this context, he made many such discoveries which were directly used in the development of industries. Many times, the owners of big factories and industries would come to him with their problems. Dr. Bhatnagar would listen to their problems very seriously and suggest solutions. Pleased with this, an industrialist gave him a huge amount. But Dr. Bhatnagar spent it to collect equipment in laboratories engaged in new scientific discoveries, so that young people could get a better chance to work.

For this reason Dr. Bhatnagar's name had spread everywhere. In 1919, after passing the examination of M.Sc. from Dayal Singh College Trust, he reached England for research work under the scholarship received After being immersed in continuous research work for three years, he received the degree of D.Sc. On his return to India, he was appointed as Professor of Physical Chemistry at the University of Lahore. But here also the research work of Dr. Bhatnakar continued. His special work was on magnetic chemistry.

In 1940, Viceroy Lord Linlithgow visited his laboratory in Lahore and was impressed by his research work. The

Government of India established the Board of Scientific and Industrial Research for the benefit of scientific research in industries. Dr. Bhatnagar was made its director. While holding this position, he made many important discoveries, which were used in the development of Indian industries. He was also aware of the technical and practical problems faced by Indian industries and used to find their scientific solutions, hence today's industrial development. He did a work of historical importance in terms of taking it to heights.

After India's Independence, he got the full support of Pandit Jawaharlal Nehru, the first Prime Minister of the country. Nehru ji was extremely impressed by Dr. Bhatnagar's scientific talent and patriotism. Dr. Bhatnagar established such a strong chain of national laboratories one after the other in the whole country, which took the country forward on the path of progress of science and played a big role in making India a superpower scientifically.

Dr. Bhatnagar had a dream that every young scientist of the country should get ample opportunities for scientific studies and research in his own surroundings. He was dreaming of a scientific India of the future, so that India would become the leading country of the world, and the scientists of the future have fulfilled it to a great extent.

This great scientist of India passed away on January 1, 1955, due to a heart attack. But whenever one looks closely at the map of India's scientific development, Dr. Bhatnagar's great contribution will automatically float in front of one's eyes.

❐

# 35

# Homi Jehangir Bhabha

## The scientist who laid the foundation of nuclear researches (1909–1966)

Homi Jahangir Bhabha's name is among the foremost scientists of the modern era, due to whom India has been able to reach the pinnacle of nuclear science. India has been able to gain fame as the world's leading nuclear power today, climbing the stairs of research one after the other, thanks to the strong foundation laid by this great visionary scientist for the nuclear program in the country. The whole world today considers India as a powerful country with nuclear power.

Homi Jehangir Bhabha was born on October 30, 1909 in a distinguished Parsi family in Mumbai. His father Jehangir H. Bhabha was a lawyer. Mother Meharbai Framji Pandey was also a highly cultured woman. After early studies in Mumbai, Homi Jehangir Bhabha went to Cambridge for higher studies, where he got the company of many eminent scientists. After returning from there, he was appointed as Reader in Physics at the Indian Institute of Science in Bangalore. But Homi's mind had a different dream.

From there, after a few years, he moved to Mumbai and became the director of a new institution, the Tata Institute of Fundamental Research. This institution was the actual form of Bhabha's dreams.

In fact, Bhabha was thinking very fast that years from now, when nuclear energy will be used to generate electricity, India should not be left behind in this field. Tata Institute of Fundamental Research was established to fulfill this dream.

In 1948, the Atomic Energy Commission was established in India, when Dr. Bhabha was made its chairman. The then Prime Minister Jawaharlal Nehru especially liked his dream of using atomic energy for peaceful purposes.

Apart from this, Bhabha's discoveries also hold important place in nuclear science. The theory of radiation energy decay by electrons and pair production by protons was such an important discovery of Dr. Bhabha, which attracted the attention of scientists from all over the world. But Bhabha's more important task is to create the capacity to build nuclear reactors in the country. Because of them, today India itself has become an important country in the world to make nuclear reactors.

Dr. Bhabha also had a keen interest in music and painting and we come across some very beautiful and artistic paintings made by him. It's surprising to know that despite devoting so much time to science, Bhabha somehow managed to find time for these interests.

This exceptionally brilliant scientist of India passed away in a plane crash on January 24, 1966. But his dream of making India a major nuclear power country is not dead. He can never die.

❐

# 36

# Vikram Sarabhai

## Famous astronomer/space scientist of India (1919–1971)

Vikram Ambalal Sarabhai is also among the scientists who have contributed the most in making India a scientifically prosperous, advanced and powerful country in the modern era. Vikram Sarabhai is counted among the top scientists of India in terms of space research. In this sense, he is one of the most respected scientists of the generation after Homi Jehangir Bhabha and one of the most loved scientists for the Indian public.

Born in an affluent Parsi family on August 12, 1919, Vikram Sarabhai was very intense, brilliant and contemplative since childhood. The family in which he was born had all facilities for reading, writing and study and Vikram was fond of reading books from the beginning. Instead of earning money, he decided to earn knowledge and work for the country. From the beginning, his interest was in mathematics and physics and he decided to make the latest discoveries while focusing on physics.

In 1943, Vikram Sarabhai went to Kashmir to study cosmic rays. But here the natural beauty of the Himalayas fascinated him so much that he thought, 'I wish I could build my own laboratory here for research on space-rays!'

However, he went to England for further research in this direction. After returning from England, he established the Physics Research Laboratory in Ahmedabad. It was also almost the same institution devoted to higher education as the institution Bhabha had created under the name 'Tata Institute of Fundamental Research', the difference was that while the institution founded by Bhabha focused more on nuclear programs and research, Vikram Sarabhai's institution centred on space research.

The truth is that from the point of view of space science, today India is counted among some of the most advanced countries in the world, the credit for this goes only to the vision, dedication and talent of Vikram Sarabhai. It was because of him that the activities of the Indian Space Research Organization (ISRO) expanded and new space technologies came to India. In 1975, the Aryabhatta satellite was sent into space. Vikram Sarabhai had the plan and idea behind this. Apart from this, he was engrossed in the study of space-rays throughout his life and his inventions and installations in this regard attracted the attention of the whole world.

In fact, Vikram Sarabhai thought that space-science is going to play a big role in the development of any nation going forward. It will be of great help to us in understanding the deep secrets of the universe, the nature of the Sun and mysteries of Nature. Along with this, it will also have its own big role in all kinds of scientific developments. In this sense, many young scientists of the new generation have done very important work by following the path shown by him by making new discoveries in space science.

Similarly, one of Vikram Sarabhai's major goals was to popularize science. He wanted that science should not be a subject of interest only to some scientists or students studying science, but the public should also take interest in it and play a big and effective role in the scientific development of the country. Only then it was possible that a talented generation of young scientists would emerge in the country, who would take India forward in that direction by connecting with the latest research happening in the world.

Apart from this, Vikram Sarabhai was in favor of modernization of many other industries such as textile, so that better results can come out of these industries and they have better construction as well as artistic perfection. So he went ahead and created many institutions. Similarly, today everyone accepts the importance of the epoch-making work of standardization done by him in the pharmaceutical industry.

This brilliant scientist, who was full of fresh enthusiasm for India, passed away at the age of 52 on December 31, 1971. We still remember him for the pivotal role he played in modern India's scientific development and in giving speed and impetus to India's space research.

The truth is that Vikram Sarabhai is also one of those who really took India to the pinnacle of science in the 21st century; despite being absent from the body, he is visible to us everywhere today in the form of a bright dream.

❐

# 37

# Har Gobind Khorana

## The one who made great discovery in genetics (1922-2011)

Har Gobind Khorana's name comes to mind first among the scientists of Indian origin living abroad who attracted the attention of the whole world with their excellent scientific discoveries and raised the flag of India far and wide. He convinced the whole world with his epoch-making discoveries in the science of genetics or genetics, stressing the fact that Indian people were not behind in knowledge or talent. If they get the right conditions and resources, they can do a lot.

Born on January 9, 1922 in Raipur village of Punjab, Har Gobind Khorana was fond of reading books since his childhood. Most of the people in the village where he was born were illiterate. Only the family of Har Gobind Khorana was educated. Initially, he studied in the village school only. He went to Lahore for further studies. After doing M.Sc. from there, he reached the University of Liverpool to do research. After getting his Ph.D. from there, when he reached home, he used to think that he would get an opportunity to work in India. He applied for a lectureship in Delhi University. But he did not get that. He was saddened by this, but not disappointed. He went to Canada and got involved in new discoveries of science. He invented a new chemical coenzyme-A, which spread his name far and wide.

From there, he came to the University of Wisconsin in America. After some time, he became Professor of Chemistry at the Massachusetts Institute of Technology. Now most of his time was spent in research on his favorite subject — genetics.

Till now the science of genetics had progressed a lot and theoretically all scientists had accepted that all living beings including humans are made of genes. These tiny genes play a decisive role in a person's personality, talent and many other things. There are innumerable such genes in every human being and animal birds, etc. It was also felt that if such genes are made artificially, then not only genetic diseases, etc. can be avoided, but also many diseases considered incurable like cancer of humans can be easily treated. Now the question was, can these genes be made in the laboratory? Because it is easy to say but more difficult to do.

But when the passionate scientist Har Gobind Khorana got involved in this work, he left everything and put all his energies in it. After all, he made and showed the gene of a bacterium named *Escherichia coli*. Gradually, he made more genes. What was surprising was that when they inserted this lab-made gene into *Escherichia coli*, it behaved exactly like other natural genes. Har Gobind Khorana was pleasantly surprised to see this. He had indeed achieved a great and revolutionary success. It was man's creative intervention in nature's creation. Within no time, Har Gobind Khorana's name became famous all over the world and he was counted among the top scientists of the world. On this discovery, he was jointly awarded the Nobel Prize in Medicine along with Marshal W. Nirenberg and Robert W. Holi. Har Gobind Khorana was then only forty-six-year old.

But even after achieving such a huge success, he did not learn to stop. He went on with further searches. His goal, like other geneticists in the world, is to eventually create the human gene, as this will truly open an unprecedented revolutionary chapter in the field of medical science.

But this task is very complicated, because the human genome is much longer and more complex than the genome of *Escherichia coli (E.Coli)*. But taking inspiration from this brilliant scientist, many scientists and many disciples of Khorana are also engaged in this work. Along with this, Khorana is engaged in the study that if some change is made in the gene, then how it affects the structure, shape and nature of an organism.

Obviously, this work of Har Gobind Khorana is as promising as it is complicated and full of dangers. But if this becomes possible, obviously, the foundation of a completely different type of medical science will be laid in the 21st century. And then Har Gobind Khorana will get the status of its epoch-making superhero. He passed away on November 9, 2011, in Concord, Massachusetts, U.S.A.

❐

# 38

## J.B.S. Haldane

### The one who immersed in Indianness
### (1892–1964)

Among the scientists of modern India, J.B.S. Haldane's name is taken with great respect. Haldane was born in Oxford, but the earthy charm of this ancient country drew him here. After coming to India, not only did he settle completely in the Indian civilization, but at the same time he contributed a lot in India's scientific progress and research.

Professor Haldane's full name was John Burden Sanderson Haldane. He was born in Oxford on 5th November 1892. His father, John Spot Haldane, was a renowned physiologist. Since childhood, John Burden was a bit mischievous but a genius. His talent would explode in new forms. Rather, sometimes he crazily did strange things. Once his mother saw him making strange postures. She was very surprised. When asked, John Burden Sanderson replied, "Mom, I'm trying to do different dog poses." After this, when he described the faces of different types of dogs, his mother couldn't stop laughing.

From a young age, Haldane became so deeply interested in science that he started helping his father in many experiments. His father was amazed to see his talent as well as his courage to play with dangers. This trend of Haldane remained till the end.

During the First World War, he worked for the country by taking many risks so much so that he used to bring important information by entering the enemy's camps.

Haldane was more interested in fauna and variety of plants. Although he was not formally educated in science, due to his deep insight, he often got to the bottom of things and used to surprise everyone with his very original type of conclusions. This originality of his discoveries in genetics attracted the attention of scientists. In 1932, he became a Fellow of the Royal Society. Haldane's wife, Dr. Helen Spunk, was also a famous scientist.

Haldane used to visit India often. This ancient country constantly attracted him because of its diversity and the wealth of its fauna and flora. Haldane was also influenced by Indianness and India's non-violence philosophy. Therefore, in 1957, he left England and came to India with his wife Dr. Helen Spurway and took citizenship here. They became so Indian that they even adopted the costumes here. He liked to wear *dhoti-kurta* and Haldane was very fond of his Indian dress.

Haldane did a lot of work in the Statistical Institute of Calcutta. Later on, he came to Bhubaneswar on the request of Orissa Government. He was made the director of the Genetics and Biometry Laboratory. He remained engaged in research here throughout his life. He finally died of cancer on December 1, 1964. Earlier he had written a wonderful poem *'Cancer is a Funny Thing'* on cancer. He knew that he had to leave soon due to cancer. But instead of being intimidated by this, he got involved in his work with more passion and enthusiasm. After Haldane's death, his wife moved to Hyderabad, where she died in 1978.

There are very few such dedicated couples in the world of science who have supported each other throughout their lives and given them strength and inspiration to move forward in their work. When Haldane came to India, his wife happily accepted his changed lifestyle and ideals and like her husband, she too immersed into Indianness.

Haldane Hall, built in the Orissa University of Agriculture and Technology, still reminds us of this heart-warming scientist, who may not have been born in India, but who was deeply rooted in Indian culture.

❐

# 39

# Ayodhya Nath Khosla

## New discovery in irrigation and water-development (1892-1984)

Ayodhya Nath Khosla's name is taken with great respect among the brilliant scientists of the early twentieth century. Especially his research work on irrigation and water development is very important and from this point of view, he is considered among the few top scientists of India.

Born in Punjab on December 11, 1892, Ayodhya Nath Khosla was very intelligent and studious since childhood. Seeing his talent, everyone was amazed and praised him. After doing B.A (honors) from D.A.V. College, Lahore, he passed the engineering examination from Roorkee. After this, he served in the several senior posts, including the Chief Engineer of the Irrigation Department in Punjab. However, his interest in the study of science and new scientific discoveries remained till the end..

Dr. Khosla worked in many branches of science and his research papers were published in the renowned research journals of the world. He also wrote many important books, which contained his research findings. Thus, he inspired the upcoming researchers for research work and acted as a good guide for them. The main work of Ayodhya Nath Khosla is related to the conservation of water flow and water resources. He seriously researched the dams being built at that time and the problems caused by them and found out their shortcomings.

According to him, instead of the water engineering method, if Bligh's Creep Theory is applied, there will be no damages to dams and their stability is increased tremendously.

Along with the difficulties arising from the flow of water in the rivers, he also did research work on the silt that settles down and put his important establishment in front of the scientists, which attracted the attention of scientists from all over the world. In this way, he found out ways to deal with the problems arising due to dams.

Taking advantage of his findings, dams were later made with modified technology and they proved to be more successful, stable and useful than before. In this way, Ayodhya Nath Khosla understood hydrology deeply and put forward new theories about it, from which scientists could communicate with him. Along with this, the general public also got special benefits. Dr. Khosla received the Shanti Swarup Bhatnagar Gold Medal in 1974 for his scientific discoveries. He was awarded the Padma Vibhushan in 1977.

Ayodhya Nath Khosla did not remain just a scientist. He also served the public for some time as a Member of Parliament. Similarly, he was the Vice-Chancellor of Roorkee University. Today, the whole world is grateful and has gratefully accepted the importance of his continuous experiments and research in liquid engineering or hydrology. For this reason Ayodhya Nath Khosla's fame will remain immortal in the future as well.

❑

# 40

# Prasanta Chandra Mahalanobis

Father of Statistics in India
(1893-1972)

Prasanta Chandra Mahalanobis was that brilliant scientist of modern India, who is remembered as the father of statistics in India. He laid such a strong foundation of statistics in India that in the last few decades, India has been considered as the leading pioneer in this field of knowledge.

Prasanta Chandra Mahalanobis was born on June 29, 1893 in a distinguished business family in Calcutta. His mother Nirodbhashini was a renowned physician. The cultured Brahmo Samaji family had such an impact on Prasanta Chandra from his childhood that he developed an urge to reach the center of the world of study and knowledge-science. After getting his B.Sc. degree from Presidency College, Calcutta, he went to Cambridge for further studies. When he came to India from there, he could not go back to London due to the First World War. He was appointed as a lecturer in the Presidency College of Calcutta. Later, he became the principal of the same college.

But despite all his hectic activities, the study of Prasanta Chandra Mahalanobis and new discoveries in the field of statistics did not stop.

Many people then considered statistics as a meaningless thing, but Rabindranath Tagore and Neelratna Sarkar encouraged him continuously and Prasanat Chandra went ahead in his passion. He felt that the coming era is the era of statistics.

In 1920, he met N. Annandale, who was then the director of the Zoological Survey of India. Annandale told Prof. Mahalanobis to make a special sociological study of the Anglo-Indian race of Kolkata with his statistical method. Prof. Mahalanobis got involved in this work with great enthusiasm. It was a wonderful opportunity for them to show the power and usefulness of statistics, and this was also a challenge. Prasanta Mahalanobis's article *'Anthropological Observations on the Anglo Indians of Calcutta'* was published after continuous study for two years. It was discussed everywhere and along with Prof. Mahalanobis, statistics also made a splash.

Despite this, statistics could not be recognized as a separate subject for a long time. Later it was included in mathematics. But with time, the usefulness of statistics increased so much and there were so many discoveries in it that finally, in 1945, statistics got the status of a separate subject.

In 1954, the then Prime Minister Jawaharlal Nehru asked Mahalanobis to study at his institute about measures to increase national income and remove unemployment. Mahalanobis did this work with great responsibility. Initially, the Institute of Statistics continued to run in the Physics Department of the Presidency College. Later, a separate building was built for it. Since then, not only this institute, but also the work and usefulness of statistics has been continuously developing. A new research unit called Biometry was opened in the institute.

It grew significantly after the arrival of Prof. J. B. Haldane and his wife, Mrs. Haldane. Similarly, psychology and linguistics research units were established. Dr. Pamela Robinson was invited from London to set up a Geological Research Unit and soon the institute became one of the model institutes of statistics in the world.

There were many such occasions when Prof. Mahalanobis underlined the utility and importance of statistics in his own way.

In 1942, there was a terrible flood in Bengal. Almost all the scientists were of the opinion that the embankments of the river should be increased. But when Prof. Mahalanobis was asked for his opinion, he collected the figures for each year. He said, arrangements should be made for smooth flow of water in the river. This opinion turned out to be absolutely correct. Similarly, he did a serious study about the rains coming in Orissa. Hirakud Dam is based on his research and it is a rare example to prove the importance of statistics.

This great scientist passed away on June 28, 1972. It was in the early decades of the 20th century that this visionary thinker understood the importance of statistics, which tis the basis of the entire development of today's India. That is why he is remembered as the pioneer of scientific progress in modern India.

❐

# 41

# Salim Ali

## Great Ornithologist of India (1896-1987)

Salim Ali was the great ornithologist of India. Rather, it should be said that Salim Ali's name comes to mind as the first among the stalwarts who has caught the attention of the whole country towards such an important study-branch as ornithology. Salim Ali had become synonymous with ornithology in India because his own life and his passion for the study of birds were not two separate things for him. In a way, he had dedicated his entire life to his great cause. This is the reason that in the field of ornithology in India, there has not been another person like Salim Ali till date. He was such an ornithologist who had no match.

For Salim Ali, the working conditions were unfavourable from the beginning. Born in a simple family on November 12, 1896, Salim Ali's full name was Salim Moizuddin Abdul Ali. Since childhood, he liked to observe animals and birds and their habits. He was also fond of hunting. Once as a teenager, he shot at a bird. That bird fell down. Then Salim Ali picked it up and started looking at it carefully. He found that bird was different from the birds he knew.

Salim's uncle was a famous hunter. Salim asked him about this bird, but he too could not tell anything specific. Then he took Salim to a place which was difficult for him to imagine. This place was the office of the Bombay History Society. He told W. M. Millard, the institute's secretary, about Salim Ali's curiosity. Millard was overjoyed to hear that. He showed them the room in which there were lying different types of birds. Actually, there were dead birds which were kept stuffed with straw. Salim was very surprised to see him. But when Millard opened a cupboard and showed him a bird similar to the one he had brought with him, Salim's joy and astonishment knew no bounds. Millard told him that this bird was a male bird of a special species.

Salim was so impressed with the institute that was opened for the study of birds that he told Millard that he would like to join it if there was any work for him. Millard told him the trick of recognizing birds. He also told how to keep the dead bird. After some time, he became a guide in the Museum of the Bombay Natural History Society and with great interest, got involved in the study of birds.

After some time, he went to Germany to learn how to stuff dead birds and keep them safe for visitors and researchers. On his return from there, he was shocked to know that the post he was working in was now over. But Salim Ali did not get discouraged. Now he had found a direction in his life and no obstacle could stop his steps.

By now he was married too and had the burden of family responsibilities on him. But his wife saw Salim's interest in birds, so she helped him a lot. She used to do the work herself so that the family could survive. Salim Ali was engrossed in the study of birds throughout the day. In his house, there were many birds. Salim Ali used to write about the shape, color, nature, etc. of these birds in a copy. Especially, he learned amazing things about birds and their nests.

He came to know that initially, the male builds these nests — not one, but many nests. Then when female likes the nest, she comes. Together they get involved in completing the nest and this nest is ready like a fine piece of art. Rest of the incomplete nests remain lying as before.

When Salim Ali wrote articles about his findings, the attention of the whole world went towards him. Similarly, Salim Ali's study about sparrow birds and his sayings are so interesting that everyone searched for that. At that time, there were no such books, which give more information about the shape, nature and living conditions of Indian birds. Therefore, fulfilling a great deficiency, he wrote his famous book *'Book of Indian Birds'* about Indian birds. Similarly, together with the famous bird lover named M. Dillon Ripley, he wrote *'Hand Book of the Birds of India and Pakistan'*. This book, which is in ten volumes, is like an important reference book about birds.

This avid ornithologist passed away on July 27, 1987, at the age of 91. But the interesting discoveries he made about birds by roaming from place to place as a nomad have now become an important part of history.

❐

# 42

# Panchanan Maheshwari

## Famous Botanist of India
## (1904–1966)

Panchanan Maheshwari was also among the scientists of the modern era who played a major role in making India a capable and advanced scientific country with their tireless hard work, talent and continuous research. He did such an important work in the field of flowering plants i.e. angiosperms that today he is considered among the pioneer scientists who have done fundamental work in this field all over the world. His discoveries and conclusions have become a guide for later generations.

Born on November 9, 1904, in Jaipur city of Rajasthan, Panchanan Maheshwari was very intelligent and studious since childhood. The condition of the family was not very good, but his father gave him the best education and he used to encourage him a lot to read and write. He used to buy him a lot of books and was very happy to see his son studying them with interest. Panchanan was very intelligent and apart from school studies, he used to take out time to read a lot. After intermediate, he went to Allahabad for further studies. There he enrolled in B.Sc. in Ewing Christian College.

There, the famous botanist Winfield Dejean was the Head of the Department of Botany. Dejean was such a visionary scientist who was always immersed in his work and liked only students who were deeply involved in their work.

When he saw Panchanan Maheshwari, he felt that this straightforward, hard-working and talented young man would go on to do a lot of work. Now Dejean, who was guiding Panchanan Maheshwari like a loving teacher, started motivating and encouraging him to continue working ahead. This instilled in Panchanan Maheshwari the urge to do more labour. He tried to live up to the test of his guru as much as possible. A unique relationship of mutual love was formed between the disciple and the teacher and the personality of Panchanan Maheshwari continued to improve.

Dejean would often take Panchanan Maheshwari out for walks in the jungles and tell him about the different types of plants and their characteristics. After this, Panchanan Maheshwari did research on angiosperms under the guidance of Dejean, which was his director's favorite subject. He studied the color, shape, embryology and their interrelationships of this group of plants. After this, Panchanan Maheshwari took forward this work and got the D.Sc. degree. As he was leaving Allahabad, his guru Dejean said, in loving words, "What I did for you, you do for your disciples."

Panchanan Maheshwari's eyes got wet after hearing this. Throughout his life, he remembered the Guru's teaching that progress in science is not achieved alone, but by working together to advance each other's work.

Panchanan Maheshwari got more than one achievements in life. In 1965, he was elected a member of the Royal Society.

He also received the Birbal Sahni Medal. When he became the Head of Botany Department at Delhi University, Panchanan Maheshwari said, echoing the words of his guru, "What I did for you, do for your disciples." And indeed he prepared many such youths for the later generation who made great and important discoveries by working on embryology.

Dr. Panchanan Maheshwari made such discoveries in the embryology of flowering plants, which no one had imagined before him.

In these, embryos of plants were to be developed in test tubes in a laboratory. A major advantage of this method was that the plants which could not be mixed with each other to form a hybrid species could now be easily converted into embryos of a new species. In this way, he made many surprising and revolutionary discoveries in the embryology of plants, which opened up innumerable directions for further work. His disciples rightly named some of these new plants discovered by the method shown by him after Panchanan Maheshwari.

This very talented botanist of India passed away on May 18, 1966, at the age of 62. But his name will always be remembered because of the useful directions he opened in botany by working in a completely distinct way.

❐

# 43

# Dr. Daulat Singh Kothari

Famous Space Scientist
(1906-1993)

Daulat Singh Kothari's name is also taken with great respect among the well-known scientists of modern India. Especially, the scientific theory he gave to understand the structure of the dwarf stars of space is considered important by almost all the cosmologists of the world. Apart from this, he wrote a book about nuclear explosions and their effects, which is considered very important even today. Dr. Kothari was one of those scientists whose scientific research was aimed at the upliftment of India and gathering resources for the service of mankind. Due to this, his status among modern scientists is very high.

Born on July 6, 1906, in Udaipur city of Rajasthan, Daulat Singh Kothari was very hard-working and talented since childhood. Due to the death of his father at a young age, he himself had to move forward and face challenges. Initially, he studied in Jaipur and Indore, then he did M.Sc. from Allahabad University.

Dr. Kothari obtained his Ph.D. degree from the University of Cambridge. But his aim was not just to get a degree. He wanted to work from the front to take India on the path of development.

Dr. Kothari was highly influenced by the eminent scientists of India namely Jagdishchandra Basu, Chandrasekhar Raman and Meghnath Saha. He had a dream that like them, he should also make India proud in the field of science.

In 1934, Dr. Kothari was appointed to Delhi University. Here, while teaching students as a professor of physics for about 25 years, he worked to generate a balanced scientific outlook and creating a deep interest in science in the minds of the next generation. After this, he was appointed in the Defense Ministry of the Government of India. After some time, he was appointed Scientific Advisor to the Defense Minister. While holding this position, he established scientific laboratories at various places in the country and carried forward scientific researches. He also encouraged research work on topics such as electronics, weaponry, methods of storing food as well as making the desert green.

Dr. Kothari inspired the scientists to work in new directions by putting forward the objective of creating a new modern India. Dr. Kothari himself discovered the pressure arcing theory, which was considered very important by scientists from India and abroad. On the basis of this principle, when he put forward his theory to understand the structure of the dwarf stars of the space, all the scientists of the world were surprised. Even today Dr. Kothari's theory related to the structure of dwarf stars is considered very important.

Similarly, Kothari did many experiments regarding nuclear fission and nuclear explosions and discovered many new things. His book *'Nuclear Explosives and their Effects'* is a very useful book in this context. Similarly, his book *'Theory of White Dwarf*

*Stars'*, written about dwarf stars, has gained a lot of respect in the scientific world. The language of Dr. Kothari is so simple that even the common man can take full advantage of it. Similarly, another notable book by Dr. Kothari is *'Numerous Papers on Statistical Thermodynamics'*.

This brilliant scientist and extraordinary educationist of India passed away on 14th February 1993, but his contribution in taking modern India to the heights of scientific development cannot be forgotten.

❐

# 44

# Dr. Atma Ram

## A Great Scientist of typical indigenous style (1908–1985)

If there is true passion in the mind, then even a child of an ordinary family can reach the top position by moving forward. The life of Dr. Atma Ram, a scientist of simple and humble nature, is an example of this. With his dedication and immense hard work, he achieved a high position in the science world and did great things. This is the reason why Dr. Atma Ram's name is taken with great respect among the talented scientists who took modern India on the path of scientific progress.

Born on October 12, 1908 in Pilana village of Bijnor district of Uttar Pradesh, Dr. Atma Ram was very curious and intelligent since childhood. His father Lala Bhagwandas was a minor Patwari, but he was honest and kind and helped everyone in the village. This had an impact on Atma Ram as well. He got good marks while doing his studies with very little money. Everyone was impressed by his interest in studies.

Still, difficulties would come again and again. Atma Ram was a very proud and lively person. He faced difficulties with great courage.

One such difficulty came when, even after passing the examination of B.Sc.in good marks, he didn't get admission in M.Sc. in Allahabad University.

This saddened Atma Ram. In those days, Dr. Neelratna Dhar was the head of the department, for whom Atma Ram had great respect. He stood outside Dr. Dhar's classroom taking notes for months after months. Then finally the Guru's heart melted and he got admission. Later, the result was out, he topped with first class. They were astonished to see that the student, who could not even get admission, secured the highest marks in the entire university.

After this, Atma Ram studied photo chemistry in depth under a scholarship which brought him the degree of Doctor of Science. Atma Ram used to lead a very simple life. This is known from the fact that out of the hundred rupees scholarship he used to get, he used to spend only seven rupees on himself and sent the rest to home.

After this, Atma Ram was appointed in the Indian Industrial Research Institute. Here he had the privilege of meeting veteran scientists like Shanti Swarup Bhatnagar and Meghnath Saha. Dr. Atma Ram also firmly decided that he would dedicate his whole life for the scientific development of the country. Here he did research on such substances which have a big role in fire-fighting. At the time of war, such fire extinguishing substances can be used to avoid the attacks of enemies. It also has emergency use in factories.

After some time, on the request of Dr. Shanti Swarup Bhatnagar, Atma Ram took over the work of Kolkata's Central Glass and Ceramic Research Institute. Here, by experimenting day and night, he succeeded in making good quality homogeneous glass (optical glass). But despite this, the Government of India wanted to import homogeneous glass from Russia. An agreement was also reached in this regard.

Then Atma Ram felt deeply sad. He wrote a letter to Prime Minister Jawaharlal Nehru, "The homogeneous glass prepared by me should be tested. If it proves to be inferior or unsuitable in any way, I will have no objection to importing homogeneous glass from abroad."

Homogeneous glass prepared by Dr. Atma Ram was tested on it and it was found to be correct and of good quality in every respect. Since then the production of fine homogeneous glass started in India. And today many such factories are working in the country. It goes to the credit of Dr. Atma Ram that today India is one of the six major countries in the world producing homogeneous glass.

But Atma Ram did not stop here. Many other types of his experiments in the field of glass also continued. He also succeeded in making fine colored glass and frothy glass. Along with this, it was his endeavor to generate interest in science in the new generation.

He observed that language is a major problem in the scientific development of India. Many talented youth hesitate to come here due to the barrier of the English language. When they read and think in their own language, they will discover new things and show them. Thinking this, he insisted on teaching and learning in Hindi. Not only this, he surprised all the scientists by reading many of his important research papers in Hindi.

Atma Ram was so simple that he never wore a tie. Once he had to go to an interview, he practiced wearing a tie for several days, but later left it forever.

This saint-heart scientist of India passed away in the year 1985. Dr. Atma Ram's name stands out among the modern Indian scientists for the fact that despite living a typical indigenous life, he did great things in science.

He showed the dream of doing the biggest work in the field of science in Hindi.

Who can forget such a simple and generous scientist!

❐

# 45

# Subrahmanyan Chandrasekhar

## Famous astronomer of India
## (1910-1995)

Subrahmanyan Chandrasekhar's name stands out like a shining star among the scientists of modern times who attracted the attention of scientists from all over the world with their discoveries in astronomy and gave many new and surprising information of historical importance in the field of stars and space science. The truth is that Subrahmanyan Chandrasekhar made space more familiar and intimate to us, opening many unsolved puzzles and mysteries of space science with his discoveries.

Born on October 19, 1910, in Lahore, Subrahmanyan Chandrasekhar was fond of reading books since childhood. He did not just read his course books, he was also interested in new discoveries in the field of physics. In this regard, wherever he got information, he used to read it with interest and think about it, so in his student life, Subrahmanyan Chandrasekhar was not only more widely read than others, but the scope of his thinking was bigger than others.

His personality was multidimensional; the one who used to accept new things from the world of life with great interest. Even in his student days, he started writing research articles and sending them to famous journals.

When he was a student of B.A. Honors at Presidency College, Madras, he had become very famous. By then many of his articles had been published in many prestigious journals. Not only his fellow students, but the teachers were also impressed by the dedication and talent of this brilliant student. Subrahmanyan Chandrasekhar reached America in connection with studies and work in 1937, when his fame as a famous astronomer had reached there too. So opportunities for study and work kept coming in front of him and Subrahmanyan Chandrasekhar completely immersed himself in his work.

Subrahmanyan Chandrasekhar's biggest and surprising discovery in astronomy is his discovery in relation to the size of dwarf stars or white dwarfs, which is today known all over the world as the 'Chandrasekhar Limit'. Subrahmanyan Chandrasekhar explained in his long research that the size of such dwarf stars cannot increase beyond a limit. Because its size is very large, there is a fierce explosion in it, due to which the excess material gets scattered and falls. Then it becomes an extremely bright, luminous supernova star, which is called a 'supernova'.

Similarly, one of his surprising discoveries is the explanation of the 'Black Holes' of space. Many found his explanation unbelievable that a black hole is such a massive astronomical object that a spoonful of its substance weighs several tons. But today almost all astronomers accept his statement. Rather, the truth is that these discoveries of Subrahmanyan Chandrasekhar have played such a big role in the correct scientific interpretation of space, which earlier people could not even imagine. In the second half of the 20th century, all the new and epoch-making discoveries related to space, somewhere in the center of them are the theory of Subrahmanyan Chandrasekhar or the important discoveries made by him. Many of his disciples are also engaged in furthering his work.

In 1983, at the age of 73, Subrahmanyan Chandrasekhar received the Nobel Prize for his discoveries in physics, even as he had already been recognized as a world-renowned astronomer several decades earlier.

Even the students who studied and got guidance from him had received Nobel Prize many decades before him. But Subrahmanyan Chandrasekhar did not give importance to it. Work was important to him and he was continuously immersed in it till the last stage of his age. Despite being such a great scientist, his life was very simple and humble and it had a deep impression of Indianness.

On August 21, 1995, this great scientist, who hoisted the flag of India in the world, passed away. The truth is that Subrahmanyan Chandrasekhar is one of those scientists, who, with his tireless hard work and discoveries, made India proud by highlighting the talent of Indians in the future.

❒

# 46

# Dr. Calyampudi Radhakrishna Rao

## Renowned Mathematician and Statistician (Born 1920)

The name of Dr. Calyampudi Radhakrishna Rao is the most important after Professor Prasanta Mahalanobis among the talented mathematicians and scientists who contributed a lot in the development of statistics in modern India. Dr. Radhakrishna Rao is one of the most able disciples of Dr. Prasanta Mahalanobis. Although it is a coincidence that he came to work in the direction of statistics and devoted his whole life to it. Actually, Radhakrishna had come to Kolkata to join the army, but seeing the Institute of Statistics here, he was so impressed that he decided to work in the field of statistics. Then he was so engrossed in it that he did one important research in this field, which created a buzz all around. His name is taken among the top statistics scholars of the world.

Born on September 10, 1920, at Dakshin Hadagali, Karnataka, Dr. Calyampudi Radhakrishna Rao was very intelligent and hardworking since childhood. His name had spread far and wide during his student days. After passing the

M.Sc. examination in Mathematics from Andhra University, he came to Kolkata. Here he studied at the Indian Statistical Institute and made many important discoveries and was sent to Cambridge by the institute, where he did his important research and got the D.Sc. degree.

After this, Dr. Calyampudi Radhakrishna Rao was the director of the Indian Statistical Institute for a long time. Many of his research papers were published in research journals of international importance. He went to Cambridge in connection with the study of the tribals of Gavil Moya of Africa and conducted his study and research on the basis of the methods discovered by his mentor Prof. Mahalanobis. Calyampudi Radhakrishna Rao believes that the use of statistics is possible even in the most advanced researches of science, which can be of great help in conducting research. However, the field of science is complex, so there is a need to be more careful about the use of statistics.

Dr. Radhakrishna Rao has done very serious work and research in the world of science. For this reason, he was made a member of the Royal Society in 1967. But it is interesting that in spite of such a serious scientific study, he is very humorous and has a lot of say in literature. He has written many beautiful satirical articles, in which his scientific and literary talent can be seen together.

Dr. Calyampudi Radhakrishna Rao considers serving the country and countrymen as his goal while living in his own country instead of getting great facilities by living abroad. Hopefully, he will continue to inspire the new generation to do some work for years to come through his research works.

❐

# 47

# H.N. Sethna

## Architect of nuclear programs (1923-2010)

H. N. Sethna is also one among the brilliant and dynamic scientists who took modern India on the path of scientific progress. Due to his incredible talent and continuous activism, he made India's name shine on the world map. He also inspired the young generation to come forward for scientific research with new zeal and enthusiasm.

Born on August 24, 1923, Homi Nusserwanji Sethna was extremely talented and passionate since childhood. He liked to read books related to knowledge and science. Even the teachers were amazed to see his talent and dedication. When he grew up, he did M.E. in the field of Chemical Engineering and many other important titles. Even after studying abroad, his mind was eager to serve the country. He believed that true knowledge or science is for the service of the country and humanity. After coming to India, Dr. Sethna was associated with the country's nuclear energy program.

India's first nuclear explosion took place in 1974 at Pokhran in Jaisalmer district of Rajasthan. This scientific achievement was achieved under the leadership of Dr. Sethna. He sent information about the success of the experiment to Prime Minister Indira Gandhi in a symbolic sentence. That was the code word, 'Buddha is coming.' Dr. Sethna chose this symbolic sentence because by this he wanted to send a message to the whole world that India's nuclear program is for establishing peace and not to destroy the peace of the world.

Buddha was a great preacher of peace and non-violence. With this, the goal and direction of India's nuclear program becomes clear in a very poetic tone.

Dr. Sethna has been associated with many important programs of scientific progress and research of India, which raised the name of India in the whole world. He showed special interest in setting up the plutonium plant at Trombay. He was elected a member of the International Scientific Advisory Committee of the Nuclear Agency. It is a matter of pride for both him and India. In 1960, he received the Shanti Swarup Bhatnagar Award and in 1975, he was awarded the Padma Vibhushan.

This hard-working and determined scientist passed away on 5th September, 2010. Till the end, Dr. Sethna was busy in completing the unfinished works of his former veteran scientists Dr. Bhabha and Vikram Sarabhai. This, in itself, is a great achievement on which the people of India are proud.

❒

# 48

## Raja Ramanna

### Icon of India's nuclear power
### (1925-2004)

Raja Ramanna is also among the scientists who have made an unprecedented contribution in making India a scientifically prosperous and powerful country in the modern era. Like the eminent scientist Homi Jehangir Bhabha, Raja Ramanna also gave push and impetus to India's nuclear programs and took Bhabha's work forward in true sense. He understood that without becoming a nuclear power, India would neither be able to accelerate its development programs nor would it be able to register its presence as a powerful country on the world map. In this sense, the way that Raja Ramanna found for the development of the country is accepted by everyone today.

Born on January 28, 1925, at Tumkur, Karnataka, Raja Ramanna was a very serious student since childhood and was interested in reading as many books as possible. He wanted to serve the country by becoming a scientist when he grew up. He went to London for research and returned with Ph.D. degree from the University there. On his return to India, the objective of his work was almost fixed. He wanted to do more and more work in the field of physics. Beginning in 1966, he became a professor at the Tata Institute of Fundamental Research, and after that the Head of the Department of Physics at the Bhabha Atomic Research Center.

Bhabha was deeply impressed by the genius, passion and dedication of this brilliant scientist. In the work he was doing regarding atomic energy, he also got the support of Raja Ramanna as a generous colleague.

Raja Ramanna had great respect for Bhabha and he found solace in doing anything for him. He also agreed with Bhabha's view that development of this continent is not possible without making the country nuclear energy rich because it is possible to use nuclear energy directly and rapidly in development works. Raja Ramanna also had full cooperation in the way Bhabha had made India a place among the major nuclear-power countries of the world by doing new research in the field of atomic energy.

When Bhabha passed away in an air crash in 1966, the whole country was immersed in a wave of mourning. Obviously, Raja Ramanna had also lost a lot along with a pioneer guide when Bhabha left, but he did not break down, did not get disheartened, rather he was determined to spend his whole life in fulfilling Bhabha's dreams.

The truth is that today India has become a country rich in nuclear weapons and behind it is the penance of Raja Ramanna. The nuclear test he conducted in Pokhran made India proud in the whole world. Along with this, a confidence came on the face of every Indian because India was no longer a scientifically backward country. The specialty of this nuclear test was that it was done inside the earth. Raja Ramanna was of the view that gunpowder is often used for digging mountains, making large ponds, dams and canals, not nuclear power. This is not right as the use of nuclear power can be more cheap and effective. But scientists used to see a danger like insecurity in it. Raja Ramanna proved through continuous experiments that the harmful effects of atomic energy can be easily controlled. Moreover, we can accomplish many big things by doing safe types of nuclear explosions.

Raja Ramanna's entire life has been devoted to the development of science.

On the one hand, he continued to worry about the progress of the country and society through his inventions, on the other, he immersed himself more and more deeply in the work of his research and experiments. In the nuclear field, he made many such inventions, which were accepted by the scientists of the whole world, and for this reason, he is discussed among the famous scientists of the world. Especially the theory of nuclear fission of an atom that he presented is considered very useful even today. Raja Ramanna believed that the heavy nucleus of an atom splits giving off very intense nuclear radiation. His discovery is considered to be of great importance in terms of nuclear fission.

This ardent and brilliant scientist passed away on September 24, 2004 in Mumbai. Today Raja Ramanna is no more, but he fulfilled the dreams of India's visionary scientist Bhabha, made the country one of the world's top nuclear power-rich countries and also suggested the path of sustainable development. Because of this, he is remembered again and again even today.

❐

# 49

# Venu Bappu

## The famous astronomer of India (1927–1982)

Among the scientists who worked tirelessly to build modern India and take it forward on the path of scientific progress, the name of the wonderful astronomer Venu Bappu will always remain immortal. He was a visionary scientist who realized the importance of astronomy years ago. By connecting India to a series of important researches being done in this direction in the world, he not only made India advanced in astronomy, but also created a desire to inspire Indian scientists to work in this direction with a different understanding and fresh enthusiasm. The truth is that these discoveries of Venu Bappu in the field of astronomy, due to which he is known all over the world today, were born from the dream or ideal of building a new India.

Born on August 10, 1927 in Chennai, Venu Bappu was very talented and inquisitive from childhood. His father used to work as an assistant in the Observatory of Hyderabad Nizam. Venu Bappu used to listen with interest not only his father's talk about the observatory, but also used to listen very carefully the words and views of the people who came from outside to give lectures on this subject.. After early studies, he went to Harvard in 1949 for higher education. Here he became friends with some famous astronomers.

Within a few days, he discovered a comet star and as a result, the attention of many astronomers turned to him. The star he discovered was also named after Bappu and his associates. The name of this comet star was Bappu-Bok-Newkirk.

After this, Venu Bappu's interest in astronomy increased further. He joined the Palomar Observatory. It was here, together with another astronomer Colin C. Wilson, that he made a new discovery, which is today known all over the world as the Bappu-Wilson theory. This theory showed that the luminosity or brightness of stars is directly related to many of their other characteristics. This was an important discovery, which helped a lot in space research. This principle is still used all over the world to find out the brightness and distance of stars.

By now Venu Bappu's name had spread far and wide, but he was determined to come to India. If he wanted, he could have got more than one lucrative position abroad, but within Venu Bappu there was a yearning to see how India progressed in the field of astronomy. Accept the challenges of working ahead by connecting with the new inventions of the world. But after coming to India, Venu Bappu was disappointed. No one took interest in his work. He didn't even get any kind of job. Despite this, instead of returning to foreign countries, Venu Bappu decided to fight by staying in India, no matter how many difficulties came in his way!

After some time, he got a job in the State Observatory of Uttar Pradesh. He attracted the attention of many by setting up a beautiful observatory on Manora peak near Nainital. Then he got a powerful telescope installed at Kodaikanal in Chennai.

As director of the Kodaikanal Observatory, he left no stone unturned to generate interest in the field of astronomy in the country. But his biggest dream was the plan to set up an extremely large and powerful telescope at Kavalur, so that this place would be known as the world's foremost astronomical center. His dream was fulfilled in 1986, when many important things and qualities were studied about the beautiful comet Heli from this observatory. Viewing the splendor of the beautiful comet Halley from this powerful telescope was a unique experience in itself.

But alas, Venu Bappu himself could not see his dream come true. He passed away on August 19, 1982, some four years before the installation of the mighty telescope, but the dream he had of making India an advanced and powerful country in the field of astronomy is still flickering in our eyes and many young scientists are busy in completing it.

In this context, the observatories built by Venu Bappu in India are not just observatories; they are such pilgrimages and temples of science, which always point towards the forward direction and do not let our steps get tired.

❐

# 50

# Dr. A.P.J. Abdul Kalam

World famous missile man
(1931-2015)

Among the dedicated and brilliant scientists of modern India, Dr. A.P.J. Abdul Kalam's name is also taken with great respect. Dr. Abdul Kalam, who is called Missile Man of India, was not only associated with country's satellite launch, but the experimental nuclear explosion in 1994 was also completed under his able guidance. Dr. Kalam's full name is Avul Pakir Jainulabdeen Abdul Kalam. Included in his name is Avul, the name of his great-grandfather, Pakir of his grandfather and Jainulabdeen of his father. A.P.J. Abdul Kalam is not only India's top scientist, but also a capable guide to take India on the path of scientific development. That is the reason why he was elected the President of India. Even today the whole public loves him with all his heart and takes inspiration from his words.

Born on October 15, 1931, in a middle-class Tamil family in Rameswaram town of Tamil Nadu, Dr. Abdul Kalam was very patient and simple since childhood and used to think all the time.

Kalam's parents were not educated, but they were simple and intelligent and there was a simple cultural environment at home. Kalam's father Jainulabdeen was a sailor.

Later on, he learned the craft of making wooden boats and started the same. Kalam was initially educated at the Rameshwaram Panchayati School, where he had many Hindu friends. Everyone lived with each other with such love that no difference was visible anywhere. Kalam was the fastest in studies. He passed his high school from Schwartz High School and intermediate from St. Joseph's College in Tiruchirappalli under very difficult circumstances at home. At the same time, curiosity to know about rockets arose in Kalam's mind. His mind was that in the future, he passed the Aeronautical Engineering examination from the Madras Institute of Technology to get to know the technology of missiles and aircraft closely. Although the financial difficulties were so much that his sister Zohra helped him by mortgaging the jewelry. Then Kalam could complete this study.

After completing his studies, Dr. Kalam was appointed as Senior Scientific Assistant in the Defense Research and Development Organization of Hyderabad. After some time, he was elected to the post of rocket engineer in the Indian Committee for Space Research. While working in this position, he established the Rocket Launching Centre, Thumba. Rohini-75 was successfully tested from here. The energetic support of Dr. Vikram Sarabhai always inspired Dr. Kalam to move forward. After the death of Sarabhai, Kalam took it upon himself to fulfill his unfulfilled dream. The Thumba campus has now been named 'Vikram Sarabhai Space Centre'. From here under the leadership of Dr. Kalam, when SLV-3 made a successful flight, the then Prime Minister Mrs. Indira Gandhi herself sent a congratulatory message and called Dr. Kalam to meet him.

After this, Kalam was made the director of the Defense Research and Development Laboratory in Hyderabad. It was from here that the completely Indian 'Devil' missile was fired. After that many missiles were successfully launched one by one, which conveyed the message of India being a capable and powerful country to the whole world. Even after retirement, Kalam remained the President of Research and Development Organisation, Hyderabad. At the same time there was a nuclear explosion in Pokhran under his leadership, due to which there was a wave of happiness all over.

After this, Dr. Kalam became the Scientific Advisor in the Ministry of Defense and finally, respecting the wishes of the whole country, he was elected the President of India. This was the first time that such a brilliant scientist was elected as the President of the country. With this, India gave a message to the whole world that it is no longer a backward country as before, but has geared up for scientific progress. In the 21st century, India is eager to reach the top.

Dr. Kalam is one of those scientists who influence the country and humanity not only through his research work but also through his personality. He showed the country a new path by lighting the torch of scientific progress all over India. For this, the generations to come will always be thankful to him.

❐

# 51

# Dr. Jayant Vishnu Narlikar

World famous astronomer of modern India

(Born 1938)

Among modern Indian scientists, the name of famous astronomer and nuclear physicist Dr. Jayant Vishnu Narlikar's place is also recognized distinctly. Dr. Narlikar is known for his space-related special studies and principles, while on the other hand, as a nuclear physicist, he has done remarkable work in advancing India's nuclear program. In this context, his name is taken with special respect among the modern scientists who have brought international fame to India in the field of knowledge and science.

Born in Kolhapur on July 19, 1938, Jayant Vishnu Narlikar received the ideological cultural environment of reading and writing at home since childhood. His father Vishnu Vasudev Narlikar was a renowned mathematician as well as the Vice Chancellor of the Banaras Hindu University (BHU). Jayant Narlikar's early education took place in Kolhapur. He went to Banaras for higher studies. Then he went to Cambridge in connection with research and his talent and sharpness impressed everyone. He did research work under the direction of Prof. Fred Hoyle, the world-renowned astronomer at Cambridge. This spread his fame across the world as a famous astronomer and astrologer. The University of Cambridge enhanced Dr. Narlikar's fame by giving him the Adam Award in the memory of Dr. Adam.

Here, Dr. Narlikar surprised the famous astronomers by giving his fundamental principles about the structure of space and stars and the birth of the universe, etc.

He believes that there are two different interpretations of the origin of the universe. But if seen, they are not that much different and somewhere they meet each other. His book *'Science, Man and the Universe'* written in this regard has gained international fame.

When Jayant returned to India after doing research on space and constellations abroad for a long time, he was appointed as a professor at the Tata Fundamental Research Institute (TFRI). But his research continued here also. For his international research, he received many prestigious awards from India and abroad, including the Venu Bappu Memorial Award. But Jayant Narlikar did not feel to blow his own trumpet. He got involved in his work with even more simplicity and simplicity.

Here, he has shown his unique talent by writing unique science stories and scientific novels. *'Explosion in Space'* and *'Virus'* are very famous in his scientific novels. In these, there are very strange fantasies of living without science in the coming times, reading which makes the mind shudder. Somewhere in these novels, Dr. Jayant is making us aware of the dangers of human's excessive dependence on science. It is good if we take the help of science to do our daily tasks easily, but if a human being becomes a slave to science and technology and his life is crippled, it cannot be called creditable in any way. These novels of Dr. Narlikar warn us about this danger.

Dr. Narlikar's another such famous science fantasy novel is *'Aagantuk'*, which has been very popular due to its unique concepts. Similarly, in his famous books *'Dhumketu'* and 'Introduction to Cosmology' are mentioned repeatedly. Dr. Narlikar has received the Birla Astronomy and Planetarium Institute Award some time back. Nowadays, through interesting writings on science, he is engaged in the work of popularizing it among the general public and generating interest in science among the young generation.

Dr. Narlikar, despite his extremely hectic schedule, still seems to be engrossed in his deep studies and research work. He has gained international fame because of his fundamental principles in astronomy. Undoubtedly, this simple and dynamic scientist has presented a great example for the coming generations.

❑❑❑